Age, Learning Ability, and Intelligence

Age, Learning Ability, and Intelligence

Edited by
Richard L. Sprott, Ph. D.
The Jackson Laboratory
Bar Harbor, Maine

VAN NOSTRAND REINHOLD COMPANY
NEW YORK   CINCINNATI   ATLANTA   DALLAS   SAN FRANCISCO
LONDON   TORONTO   MELBOURNE

Van Nostrand Reinhold Company Regional Offices:
New York   Cincinnati   Atlanta   Dallas   San Francisco

Van Nostrand Reinhold Company International Offices:
London   Toronto   Melbourne

Copyright © 1980 by Litton Educational Publishing, Inc.

Library of Congress Catalog Card Number: 80-13140
ISBN: 0-442-27895-0

All rights reserved. No part of this work covered by the copyright hereon may be reproduced or used in any form or by any means—graphic, electronic, or mechanical, including photocopying, recording, taping, or information storage and retrieval systems—without permission of the publisher.

Manufactured in the United States of America

Published by Van Nostrand Reinhold Company
135 West 50th Street, New York, N.Y. 10020

Published simultaneously in Canada by Van Nostrand Reinhold Ltd.

15 14 13 12 11 10 9 8 7 6 5 4 3 2 1

Library of Congress Cataloging in Publication Data

Main entry under title:

Age, learning ability, and intelligence.

Includes indexes.
  1. Learning, Psychology of. 2. Intellect.
3. Aged—Psychology. 4. Aging—Psychological aspects.
I. Sprott, Richard L. [DNLM: 1. Aging. 2. Intelligence. 3. Learning. BF433.A3 A265]
BF318.A35   155.67   80-13140
ISBN 0-442-27895-0

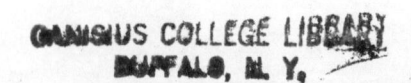

Contributors

David Arenberg, Ph.D., National Institute on Aging, Gerontology Research Center, Baltimore City Hospital, Baltimore, Maryland

Merrill F. Elias, Ph.D., Department of Psychology, University of Maine, Orono, Maine

Charles L. Goodrick, Ph.D., National Institute on Aging, Gerontology Research Center, Baltimore City Hospital, Baltimore, Maryland

Elizabeth A. Robertson-Tchabo, Ph.D., Department of Human Development, University of Maryland, College Park, Maryland

K. Warner Schaie, Ph.D., Andrus Gerontology Center and Department of Psychology, University of Southern California, Los Angeles, California

Richard L. Sprott, Ph.D., The Jackson Laboratory, Bar Harbor, Maine

Preface

The last decade has seen a tremendous surge of interest in gerontology, particularly behavioral gerontology. The creation of the National Institute on Aging in 1974 is a concrete symbol of our growing concern with the phenomena of aging and senescence. With this surge in interest have come an increase in data and a concomitant increase in debate about the meaning of the new data. The purpose of this volume is to focus on one area of debate, the area of learning and cognitive abilities, by presenting a variety of points of view in a single format. While there are many areas of disagreement among the contributors, we all hope we have eliminated our superficial differences and have thereby presented as concise a view as is presently possible of the current state of knowledge for a very complex set of questions.

Richard L. Sprott

Acknowledgments

My sincere appreciation must be extended to those who made this book possible: Ms. Barbara Dillon for typing every draft and keeping track of every detail of organization, Mrs. Jane Harris for her hours in the library, Dr. Sherman Ross for his encouragement and advice at every stage of preparation, and finally each of the contributors and their staffs for their labor and their ideas.

Contents

Preface		vii
1:	Introduction Richard L. Sprott	1
2:	Problem Solving and Age: A Critique of Rodent Research Charles L. Goodrick	5
3:	Senescence and Learning Behavior in Mice Richard L. Sprott	26
4:	Age Changes in Intelligence K. Warner Schaie	41
5:	Disease, Aging and Cognition: Relationships between Essential Hypertension and Performance Merrill F. Elias	78
6:	A Behavior-Genetic Approach to the Study of Age, Hypertension and Behavior: Testing the Non-Causality Hypothesis Merrill F. Elias	114
7:	Age Differences and Age Changes in Cognitive Performance: New "Old" Perspectives David Arenberg and Elizabeth A. Robertson-Tchabo	139
8:	Summary Richard L. Sprott	158
Index		165

Age, Learning Ability, and Intelligence

1
Introduction

Richard L. Sprott

The Jackson Laboratory
Bar Harbor, Maine

Most of us have an elderly relative or acquaintance whom we admire for his or her "extraordinary" mental abilities, and we hope to be in the same shape when we achieve a comparable age. Unfortunately, we also have an intuitive feeling that the odds on realizing this hope are not good, since we also have elderly relatives and acquaintances who are forgetful, rigid, or worse. Which are the "extraordinary" individuals, those who function well until they die (or at least reasonably close to that point) or those who show a gradual loss of all of their faculties from middle age onward? That question, phrased in many guises, is the raison d'être for this book. There is no simple answer, and one can make a strong case for the "normalcy" of either pattern of aging, as you will see in subsequent chapters.

There is an unstated argument which underlies the diversity in opinion about the natural course of learning ability and intelligence over a life span, the nature of the aging process. If aging is itself a "disease" process, then its effects should be seen in all individuals as they age. If, on the other hand, aging is a reflection of the cumulative effects of various disease states, then considerable variation in the effects will be seen in any population of individuals. While this difference in assumptions is commonly avoided by simply referring to the effects of the passage of time as aging (these effects can be positive, negative or neutral) and to deleterious changes which occur after middle age as senescence, the assumptions are still there. Behavioral research is not going to settle this issue, but it will benefit greatly from the biological research being conducted in many laboratories which does address the issue. Meanwhile, behavioral gerontologists will continue to probe the limits of animal and human abilities throughout the life span and to describe the conditions which affect these limits.

The primary concern of studies of learning ability in aging animals and of cognitive ability and intelligence in aging human groups is whether loss of such functions is a gradual process that begins shortly after a peak during a "prime" period of maturity, or whether it occurs as a consequence of loss of physiological functions from the degenerative diseases which appear with increased frequency in aging organisms. The two points of view are not mutually exclusive, and in fact both patterns of change appear to be common. Sensory and motor skills decline gradually, while some learning abilities remain intact throughout the life span of most subjects (mice or men). The contributors to this volume are all involved in research in the difficult "middle ground," where the pattern of age change varies from one individual to another. It is this individual variation that makes sincere difference of opinion the norm and that promotes the sometimes obsessive concern with methodology which characterizes the field. At the same time, it is this same individual variation that gives hope and meaning to the research, since it provides a constant source of examples of what we might achieve if we could preserve the abilities of most individuals at levels comparable to those observed in today's "extraordinary" examples.

In order to achieve this aim we must first separate certain influences upon behavior so that we can assess the role each plays in the course of behavioral development over the life span. The major influences are ability, by which we mean the biological capacity of the organism to respond to stimuli; health status, which can affect both ability and performance; and the expectations of society, which clearly affect performance and may affect ability as well. Each of these influences is discussed at length in subsequent chapters, sometimes to what seems an excessive degree. However, at this stage in the development of our research this emphasis is unavoidable. In order to understand, and perhaps even modify, the biological necessities of aging, we must first eliminate factors which are not causally linked to aging per se. In the process we should be able to contribute substantially to the well-being of elderly individuals by clearly delineating the effects of factors like health status, cultural expectation, and motivation and thereby suggest strategies to ameliorate their consequences. What we seek is not to lengthen life, but rather to improve the odds that each of us fortunate enough to live to a ripe old age may do so with intelligence and dignity.

Each of the chapters in this volume deals with some aspect of the learning ability/intelligence problem. Both terms, learning ability and intelligence, are theoretical constructs, not entities which can be accurately measured with complete agreement. Part of the difficulty of assessing age-dependent changes in abilities and intelligence derives from lack of agreement about what it is we are measuring. Lower animals have the ability to learn a variety of tasks and to solve many problems. However, the sum of the abilities of any species (with the possible exception of chimpanzees and dolphins) does not produce an intelligence which approaches that of human beings. Human intelligence is a construct (or set of constructs) to categorize and quantify the sum of human abilities which, when considered together, describe the ability to function in human societies. We have no comparable constructs for lower animals. Therefore, research on aging involving lower animals is confined to research on specific abilities. Research with human subjects includes specific abilities research, but is often extended to assess the relationship of specific abilities to intelligence. The assumption that the sum of human abilities is more than its parts is central to research on age relationships to intelligence, just as it is to other areas of intelligence research. The consequence of this assumption for the development of human research questions and conclusions is discussed later (Chapter 4). The consequence for comparative research with lower animals is to lead many investigators to believe that in lower animals, also, the sum of abilities may be more than its parts. This assumption in turn leads to questions of how to measure the sum. Appropriate measures might include tasks of increasing complexity or tests of ability to extract principles from a series of simple tasks. Some investigators argue that it is impossible to conduct an adequate test in the protected environment of the laboratory, that survival in a "natural environment" is the measure we should use. The "natural environment" argument has a certain appeal, except for the fact that few, if any, of the lower animals used for research on aging survive beyond early maturity in their natural environment. We cannot observe the effects of senescence in such situations.

Since we cannot measure senescent changes in ability to function in a natural environment, we are forced to do so in the laboratory. There we have far better control of the variables which affect longevity as well as those which affect performance, but we may never be sure of the importance of our measures as they relate to survival ability. Does it, in fact, matter? Probably not, since our real interest is not whether mice or rats become senile in their burrows, but whether they show any senescent changes in abilities. We can use the insights gained from answering these questions to help solve the methodological problems of similar human research and to increase our understanding of general principles of mammalian aging.

The research presented in subsequent chapters is descriptive in the sense that we have attempted to assess the current status of knowledge about senescent changes, or lack thereof, in learning abilities and intelligence. We have not attempted to answer questions about "biological clocks" or genetic aging programs. A plethora of hypotheses to explain aging processes already exists. What we have attempted to accomplish is to present what is known with reasonable certainty and to suggest ways to acquire the information which we do not yet have. Research on learning abilities and intelligence in mature and senescent organisms is an important endeavor in its own right, whether or not it contributes to an understanding of the "causes" of aging. Our aged population is large and growing, and no intelligent society can afford to waste the abilities of 20% of its population. To do so for reasons of political or economic expediency would be criminal, while to do so for lack of research effort would be no less than tragic.

2
Problem Solving and Age: A Critique of Rodent Research

Charles L. Goodrick

National Institute on Aging
Gerontology Research Center
Baltimore City Hospital
Baltimore, Maryland

INTRODUCTION

The purpose of this review is to provide information regarding procedures which are necessary to analyze the learning process of rats. Learning studies of aged rats and young rats (and selected studies of mice) are reviewed and some of the difficulties inherent in such research are discussed.

MAZE LEARNING

The Stone Monographs

A major set of studies relating to age and animal learning in rats was published in 1929 by Calvin Stone in two separate monographs (Stone, 1929a, b). After this substantial effort, Stone never published any further research on the topic. He published for at least 20 more years, but did most of his research in the analysis of rat sexual behavior. This might be expected because Stone's learning studies with rats of different ages were negative. He studied learning in rats at ages from 1 to 24 months, with young rats allowed to gain weight over the course of each experiment and aged rats fed less to cause a reduction in weight over the course of each experiment. Tests used included simple lever-escape and three plate-escape problems, the Carr maze (17 units), the 14-unit T-maze, a multiple light discrimination, and a very difficult maze. Stone's conclusion was the following: "The level of maximum learning rate in all probability does not decline in normal animals having no interference habits throughout the first two-thirds or more of their life span, i.e., during the first two years of life" (Stone, 1929b, pp. 195–196).

In reviews of early research, Munn (1950, p. 351) accepted Stone's conclusion, but others have insisted that age differences were obtained by Stone (Jerome, 1959; Botwinick, 1973). Botwinick's otherwise excellent review of gerontological research, for example, suggested that Stone found aged rats were more rigid than young rats in Stone's very first experiment (Stone, 1929a). In fact, Stone found that immature rats were so active in the simple lever-escape problems that they would accidentally "solve" the problem faster than mature rats during early trials; these immature rats actually *increased* learning time over trials. Interestingly, on the last two trials (out of 20), the oldest, 2-year-old, group solved the problem faster than any other age group. Although Jerome (1959) noted that no age differences were obtained in the 14-unit T-maze or the Carr maze, he suggested that during relearning the Carr maze ". . . The 2-year-old animals show a marked impairment of retention which is statistically reliable" (p. 685). Actually the age differences for the Carr maze relearning data were not very impressive. At the beginning of relearning, the oldest rats averaged about 1.0 errors per day, and at the end of relearning about 0.5 errors per day. The error performance of the youngest groups averaged slightly below that of the 2-year-old group. Considering all of the Stone experiments, it is apparent that for these rat populations, age differences in learning ability were not obtained. Jerome (1959, pp. 644–675) gives an excellent summary of these studies, including type of problem, age and number of animals, type of deprivation, and results.

Three of Stone's very important major methodological conclusions (1929b, pp. 195–199) were:

1. Maximal level of motivation should be attained for all animals. [Stone used differential deprivation, that is, older animals were placed on a feeding regimen such that they slowly lost weight, while younger animals slowly gained weight. The result was high motivation for all rats.]
2. Test instruments must be carefully chosen so that a measure of learning is obtained which is independent of speed of response.
3. These results hold only for the first two-thirds of the life span of the rat. [The rats used by Stone were obtained from J. R. Slonaker and these rats had an average life span of about 3 years (Slonaker, 1907), different from many present laboratory rat populations which have an average life span of about 2 years (Schlettwein-Gesell, 1970).]

Multiple-Discrimination Learning

Fields (1953) studied the age factor in multiple-discrimination learning by rats. The rats used in this study, 1 month old and 15 months old, were maintained at 80–85% of starting weight and were tested in a two-choice visual discrimination test which required the rat to jump to the correct visual stimulus displayed on one of two cards. Although young and old rats did equally well in a simple test of visual discrimination, the older group did significantly less well than the younger group in a multiple visual discrimination test.

This study has the three methodological deficiencies discussed in the preceding section. Motivation was differential in relation to age, as Stone suggested, but was differential for the wrong age group. In Fields' study, the young rats were maintained at just over 50 grams of body weight, an extremely low level, while the older rats were maintained at about 325 grams. In Stone's studies, 1-month-old rats were allowed some weight gain. The test used had both a time component and an error component, so the error component may be an accurate measure of learning, but this is an unusual test which requires a jumping response. This type of response may be easier for a rat 1–3 months old (very low in body weight) than for an older and heavier rat. The ages selected by Fields, 1–3 and 15–16 months, represent immature and mature-old rats. Fields correctly described these groups as young and middle-aged. In order to be considered aged, Sprague-Dawley rats (the stock used by Fields) should be from 23 to 25 months old. Therefore, conclusions regarding the learning ability of old rats cannot be made.

The Verzar-McDougall Study

Verzar-McDougall (1957) used rats aged 2–3 months, 8–9 months, 12–18 months, 20–27 months, and 30 months. These rats were reduced in body weight to about 80% of their starting weight over the 30 days of the experiment, when each rat was tested daily in the Stone 14-unit multiple T-maze. The proportion of rats which failed to learn the maze in 26 trials became greater with increasing age: 2–3 months old, 7/40; 8–9 months old, 2/43; 12–18 months old, 6/20; 20–27 months old, 19/42; and 30 months old, 10/12.

In this study, the test choice was excellent, and the ages represented a complete range from very young to very old. The 50% mortality point for aged females is about 26 months for this population (Schlettwein-Gesell, 1970), so the oldest group, twelve 30-month-old female rats, was very old. However, the motivation procedures for these rats were possibly inadequate. The procedure of reducing the weight of all rats by 20% may result in young rats which are more highly motivated than old rats. It may have been difficult to maintain individual rats at their specific weights, as the rats were fed in groups of five once daily at the end of the maze in a goal box. It is possible that the older rats were less motivated than the young rats. Verification of this hypothesis requires that old rats remain slow in moving from the start to the end of the maze during later trials. This result was reported by Verzar-McDougall (1957) with 10 of the 12 oldest rats taking 2 to 7 minutes to pass through the maze. Properly motivated rats of all ages will move through the maze in less than 30 seconds (e.g., Goodrick, 1968).

The Kay and Sime Studies

Kay and Sime (1962) studied food-deprived hooded rats in tests where the rat pushed aside one of a pair of perceptual stimuli to obtain a food reward. The rats were mature-young (5–10 months old) and mature-old (15–23 months old) and were motivated by restricting feeding to a period after testing of about 1 to 3 hours. After learning to a criterion, the positive stimulus was switched to negative, and vice versa. This reversal of the positive cue occurred five times in one experiment, and 15 times in a second experiment. There were no age differences in learning or reversal learning. Sime and Kay (1962) obtained similar results in a second experiment.

In these experiments, the degree of subject motivation is not clearly defined because neither body weights nor the amount of food provided was reported. Also, the tests used were too simple for an analysis of the learning process, and resulted in very fast learning even during many reversals. Aged animals were not included in these studies; therefore, no conclusions are possible concerning changes in learning ability during the late stages of the life span.

The Botwinick, Brinley, and Robbin Studies

These studies (Botwinick, Brinley, and Robbin, 1962, 1963) were specifically designed to test the hypothesis that aged rats are behaviorally more rigid than young rats; that is, aged rats would have greater difficulty reversing a learned habit than young rats. In two experiments post-pubescent, middle-aged, or aged rats were fed once a day, then tested in a Y-maze discrimination task and discrimination-reversal tasks (Botwinick, Brinley, and Robbin, 1962). No age group differences were observed in learning or reversal learning of the Y-maze discrimination. A further study (Botwinick, Brinley, and Robbin, 1963) found age differences in learning a four-choice Y-maze, but not in reversal learning of the same task. Original learning occurred more slowly with increasing age.

These studies used appropriate age groups: post-pubescent rats were 3–4 months old, middle-aged were 8–14 months old, and old were 21–30 months old, completely encompassing the adult age range for the Sprague-Dawley rat. Motivation was not well defined; although relative body weight was discussed (1962, p. 319), the exact feeding schedule was unclear. Also, the tests used were too simple to adequately study the learning process or reliably determine differences between groups.

AVOIDANCE LEARNING

In tests of avoidance learning, electrical shock is used as the motivator for learning. Movement of the animal may be required to avoid the shock (active-avoidance) or inhibition of movement by the animal may be required to avoid the shock (passive-avoidance). Early in the history of this type of test, Yerkes and Dodson (1908) studied the relation of strength of stimulus to rapidity of habit formation. The law formulated from that study was given by Yerkes in 1910 (p. 253).

> The law which is indicated by these facts may be formulated thus. *As difficultness of visual discrimination increases that strength of electrical stimulus which is most favorable to habit-formation approaches the threshold. The easier the habit the stronger that stimulus which most quickly forces its acquisition; the more difficult the habit the weaker that stimulus which most quickly forces its acquisition.*
>
> This consideration makes apparent the incomparability of the results of the plasticity experiments. Instead of uniformity and simplicity of conditions, we have variability and complexity. It is evident that before a given individual can be used to advantage in any such training experiments as these, or rather before we can interpret the results, we must know accurately the relations of the conditions of experimentation to the individual.

The preceding paragraphs indicate considerable complexity with respect to the interpretation of experimental results. But, nevertheless, Yerkes insists that ". . . I do not regard the results of the . . . experiments as valueless" (1909, p. 254). The two factors of test unreliability and lack of validity result in an incredible garble of results (1909, pp. 269–270):

1. The dancer [mouse] at one month of age acquires a particular white-black visual discrimination habit more rapidly than do older individuals. From the first until the seventh month there is a steady and marked decrease in rapidity of habit-formation; from the seventh to the tenth month the direction of change is reversed. These statements hold for both sexes.
2. Young males acquire the habit more quickly than young females, but between the ages of four and ten months (at least) the females acquire the habit the more quickly.

3. Curves of learning for the sexes indicate that the female makes more mistakes early in the training tests than does the male, but that this condition soon gives place to greater accuracy of choice on the part of the female. . . .

Sprott (1972) worked with young mice of two ages (5 weeks old, and 4–5 months old) in a passive-avoidance conditioning test. The test required staying in a safe area to avoid shock for a specified period of time. Such a test may favor older mice, because activity of mice decreases with increasing age (Goodrick, 1975a), and in this test, increasing inactivity over trials is considered learning. In fact, it was found that performance was a function of age, strain, and shock intensity. The problem posed for the mouse required little problem-solving skill because most of the mice learned the problem within three to seven trials (64 of 81 mice had reached criterion on the third trial). It was indicated in the previous section that such simple tasks were not appropriate either for an analysis of the learning process or for the study of age differences in learning (Stone, 1929a, b). Sprott and Stavnes (1975) reviewed the avoidance-conditioning/aging literature to determine why this system had failed to provide new information concerning the learning process and aging. One conclusion was that the fault was in the investigators' failure to assess the adequacy of their subjects. This is certainly correct (see statements of Yerkes), but the test itself may also be a prime problem. In presenting his later work on passive-avoidance conditioning and aging of mice 5 weeks to 30 months old, Sprott (1978) comments: "Now it is clear that advancing age has little or no effect, beyond the early maturation period, upon performance in this situation" (p. 116). He concludes: ". . . it could be argued that our tests are not complicated enough to reveal any learning ability decrement that may exist" (p. 119). This is probably a correct assessment.

Doty and co-workers have published a series of experiments using active-avoidance conditioning tasks with rats (e.g., Doty, 1966). In her studies, rats were required to run to a lighted compartment of an apparatus within 5 seconds of the appearance of a light in order to avoid shock. In these studies, the older rats may be at a disadvantage because aged rats are normally less active than young rats (Slonaker, 1912; Doty and Doty, 1967). In addition, senescent rats avoid lighted areas much more than young rats (Goodrick, 1971), and senescent rats are more emotional than young rats (Doty and Doty, 1967; Goodrick, 1971). Doty and O'Hare (1966) also found that older rats improved in shock-avoidance performance more than young rats as a function of increased shock intensity. The hypothesis that age differences in avoidance-learning tests are related to age differences in emotionality rather than age differences in learning ability was dramatically confirmed in a study in which handled aged rats "learned" as quickly as young rats, while nonhandled aged rats "learned" more slowly than young rats (Doty, 1968). Handling may act to reduce the emotionality of "emotional" old rats to a greater degree than relatively "unemotional" young rats.

The rat studies of Doty and the mouse studies of Sprott are both examples of the difficulty of test selection and the trap of using a performance measure of learning, whether it be active or passive. In a test situation where fear is a motivation factor and populations are studied which differ in emotionality, activity, and shock threshold, it is my belief that learning or memory processes of these groups cannot be clearly differentiated and subjected to analysis.

LATER MAZE STUDIES

A series of studies have been completed which: (a) use animals appropriate to determine age differences (e.g., mature-young vs. senescent rats at or past the 50% point of mortality, (b) use differential motivation (the senescent rats are more highly motivated than the young rats), and (c) use tests which are of adequate complexity to allow the detection of age differences in learning and also allow an analysis of the learning process (Goodrick, 1968, 1972, 1973a and b, 1975b).

In an initial study, Goodrick (1968) tested male and female Wistar rats in the Stone 14-unit T-maze (Figure 2.1) at 6 months of age and 26 months of age (senescent). Both young and senescent rats were reduced in body weight progressively over the duration of the experiment, but the body weight of senescent rats was reduced to a greater degree than the body weight of young rats (Table 2.1). The rats were tested for 10 days with four training trials per day, with 60 to 80 minutes between trials. It is important to note that all rats were

Problem Solving and Age 13

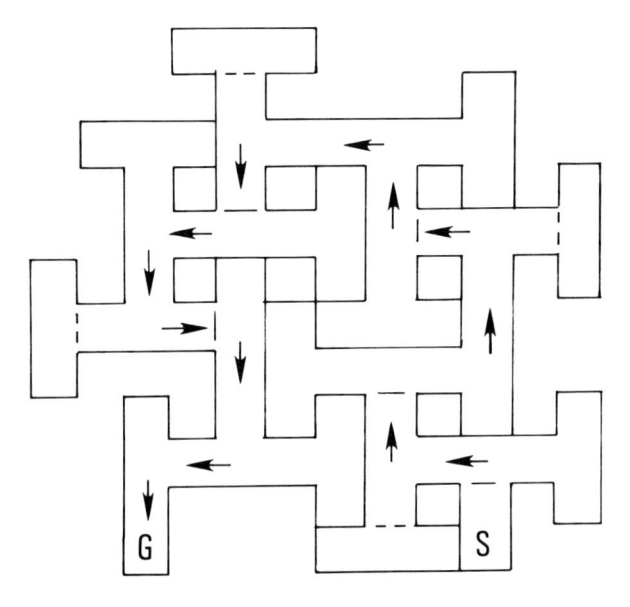

Figure 2.1. Modified Stone 14-unit multiple T-maze. Dimensions: 150 cm × 150 cm; 12.5 cm wide; 45 cm high. Door = —; dummy door = — —; goal = G; start = S.

Table 2.1. Mean Weights and Proportions at Three Stages of the Experiment.*

	YOUNG MALE	YOUNG FEMALE	SENESCENT MALE	SENESCENT FEMALE
	WEIGHTS (TOTALS IN GRAMS)			
Ad Libitum	441.1	240.6	472.8	327.8
(a)	359.2	190.8	356.7	250.4
(b)	340.4	178.6	334.8	233.8
(c)	329.7	178.6	332.2	227.3
	WEIGHTS (% OF ORIGINAL BODY WEIGHT)			
(a)	81.4	79.6	75.4	74.7
(b)	77.3	74.6	70.9	71.3
(c)	74.9	74.8	70.4	69.3

NOTE: (a) = start of training; (b) = end of training; (c) = end of all tests.
* Goodrick, 1968.

adapted to the reward solution on a series of preliminary tests both in the home cage and in a straight runway. Also, in order to minimize the performance component of learning, the error score was used as the criterion of learning, rather than the time score. The criterion for mastery of the maze was four errors or less during the four daily trials. Over the 10 days of testing, 23 out of 24 mature-young rats attained this criterion, while only 18 out of 36 senescent rats attained this criterion. Many of these aged rats which failed to reach criterion did not reduce error scores over the last days of testing. These rats were called slow-learning senescent rats.

For a more complete study of the learning process, the original learning sheets for each trial were analyzed in detail. These sheets are maps showing the exact path of each rat on every trial (see Figure 2.1). Ten rats were randomly selected from each of three groups: (a) mature-young rats, (b) senescent rats which reached criterion, and (c) senescent slow-learning rats. For trials 5–16, 17–28, and 29–40, wrong turns were tabulated for each choice point (just one counted per trial for each choice point). It was found that senescent slow-learning rats tended to repeat errors or perseverate at specific choice points more than senescent rats which reached criterion, or mature-young rats. In order to quantify perseverative behavior, a criterion was set of 10 or more errors at the same choice point during a set of 12 consecutive trials.

Examples of records of the first six choice points for typical animals of each group are given in Table 2.2. All of the senescent slow-learning rats made perseverative errors, while only five of the senescent rats which reached criterion and one mature-young rat made perseverative errors ($\chi^2 = 7.64$, df $= 2$, $p = < 0.05$).

Twelve slow-learning senescent rats completed an additional series of tests in which the distribution of practice was varied. The results for these senescent slow-learning rats which continued training are shown in Figure 2.2. Because massed practice is thought to be related to poor learning performance (e.g., Kimble, 1961, p. 125), it was decided that one trial per day rather than four per day might result in a reduction of errors. A series of 12 daily single trials failed to result in a reduction of errors for this group; therefore, it was decided to try highly massed practice. Each rat of the senescent slow-learning group ($n = 12$) was tested with the following procedure: 12 trials

Table 2.2. Number of Errors Made at the First Six Choice Points During 12 Trial Segments of Learning for One Randomly Selected Rat from Each Group.*

CHOICE POINT	SENESCENT SLOW LEARNING RAT			SENESCENT FAST LEARNING RAT			YOUNG RAT		
	(A)	(B)	(C)	(A)	(B)	(C)	(A)	(B)	(C)
1	9	9	12	6	10	3	6	4	0
2	10	8	4	7	4	0	4	0	1
3	10	10	10	12	5	0	4	2	0
4	4	1	0	2	0	0	2	0	0
5	9	7	1	7	1	0	6	0	1
6	2	0	0	10	2	0	5	1	0

NOTE: (a) = 1st 12 trials; (b) = 2nd 12 trials; (c) = 3rd 12 trials.
* Goodrick, 1968.

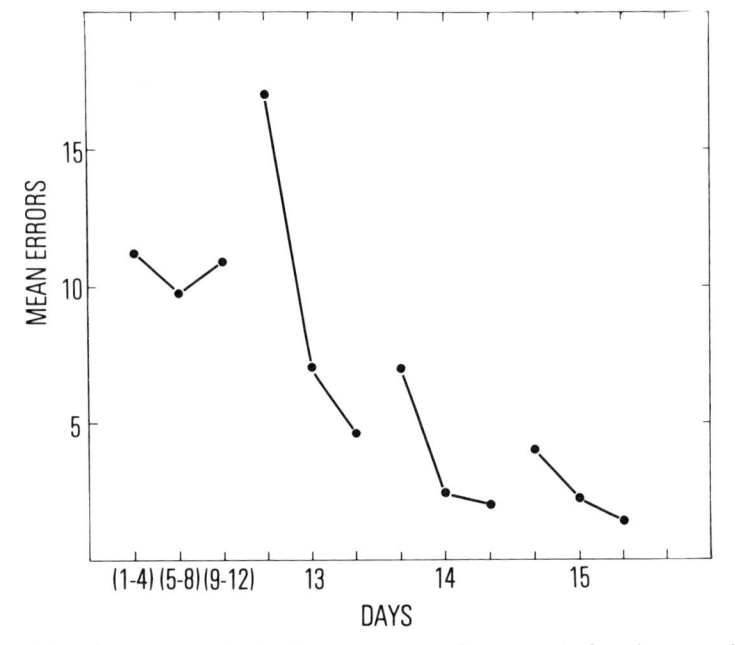

Figure 2.2. Mean errors obtained for a group of senescent slow learners during distributed (days 1–12) and massed (days 13–15) practice on 15 days following training. Each point represents the mean score for 4 trials.

16 Age, Learning Ability, and Intelligence

were given on each of three days, four trials consecutively with 90 minutes between each four-trial block. Using this procedure, the mean errors initially increased, then decreased dramatically. At the end of the series of 36 trials, the mean number of errors was two for the four-trial block, or 0.5 errors per trial, with 11 out of 12 rats reaching the criterion of four or fewer errors per four-trial block.

The major findings of this experiment were: (1) clear age differences in problem-solving ability, (2) the persistence of aged rats in making the same errors repeatedly over trials, and (3) a dramatic reduction of errors of aged slow-learning rats when allowed highly massed practice.

Goodrick (1972) published a concurrent study several years later. In this study, four different test situations were used which varied in complexity. In simple tests, such as the straight runway or the 1-unit T-maze, age differences in learning were not observed. Senescent rats did as well as mature-young rats on these tests. In a more complex four-point problem senescent rats made significantly more errors than mature-young rats, but the largest between-group differences were observed on the first trial of a new problem-learning sequence. This may indicate a greater difficulty of adaptation to new learning situations for senescent rats than for mature-young rats, rather than reduced learning ability for senescent rats compared with mature-young rats. These age differences in learning ability, using mazes of moderate complexity, need to be studied in greater detail in long-term research projects. The 14-unit T-maze was also used to replicate the finding of age differences obtained earlier (Goodrick, 1968). The distributed practice procedure (one trial per day) was used in order to ensure maximal age differences. Prior to testing, all rats were carefully gentled and pretested in the straight runway. The animals used were mature-young and senescent male rats (6 and 26 months old, $n = 16$ per group), with the senescent group reduced in body weight to a greater degree than the mature-young group. The exact path of each rat was plotted on every trial as in previous studies. The mean error scores are given in Figure 2.3 for the 20 daily test trials. The senescent rats made a similar number of errors on the initial trials, but by the last trials there were reliable between-group differences, with young rats making significantly fewer errors than aged rats [all ts (30) < 2.75, $p < 0.01$]. On trial 20, 15 out of 16 mature-young

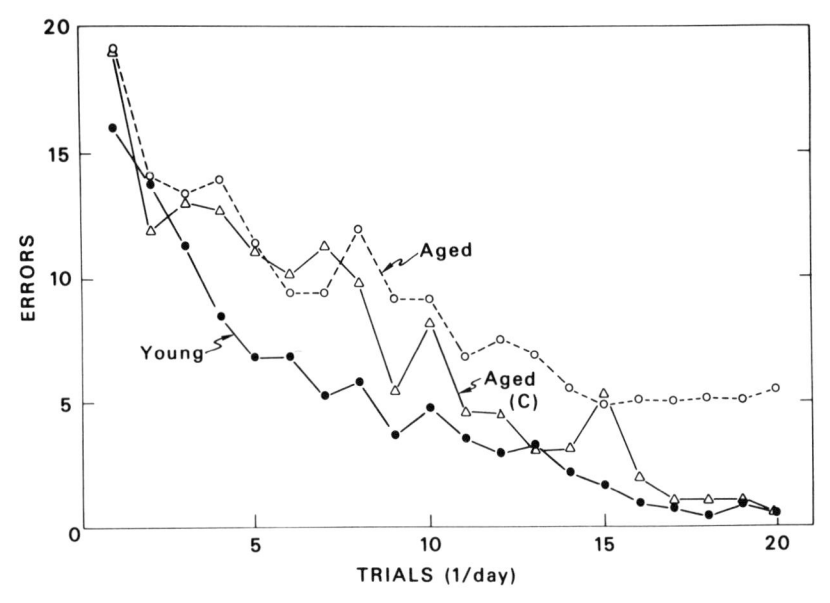

Figure 2.3. Mean errors obtained by mature-young and aged rats during 20 daily tests in a 14-unit T-maze. Group C represents aged rats which learned the maze.

rats had one or no errors while 6 out of 16 aged rats had one or no errors. As shown in Figure 2.3, these six senescent rats which reached criterion (group C) were not equivalent in performance to the mature-young group until the last trials. Perseverative errors were also made more frequently by aged-senescent rats than by mature-young rats. Age differences in percentage of choice points where six consecutive errors were made were highly significant statistically [t (30) = 3.86, $p < 0.001$]. Mature-young rats made this type of repetitive error sequence on 16.2% of the possible occasions, while aged-senescent rats made this repetitive error sequence on 47.1% of the possible occasions. Figure 2.4 shows the record for two rats. The mature-young rat made numerous errors, but did not make any sequences of six consecutive errors at any of the 14 choice points, while the aged senescent rat made clear perseverative responses at choice points 2, 3, and 11. This study clearly demonstrates that reliable age differences in learning may be obtained under conditions of differential motivation using the 14-unit T-maze. The distributed practice condition is also necessary where positive rewards are used, with one trial per day an appropriate con-

18 Age, Learning Ability, and Intelligence

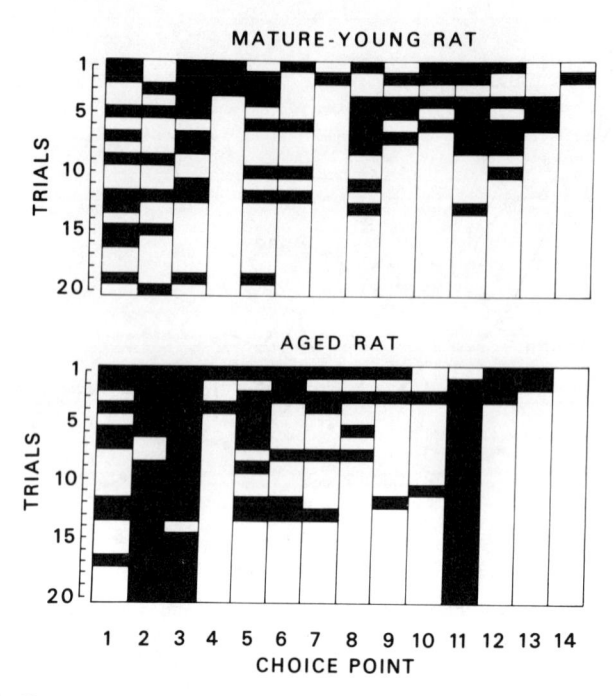

Figure 2.4 Errors made by a representative mature-young rat and a representative aged rat as a function of trials and maze choice-point.

dition to show age deficits in a high percentage of aged rats. In addition, this test demonstrates reliable persistent perseverative responses in many aged-senescent rats, responses which could be studied experimentally.

Goodrick (1973a) conducted a further study specifically designed to examine distribution of practice of mature-young and aged-senescent rats tested in the 14-unit T-maze. As in previous studies, all rats were carefully gentled and adapted to the test situation. During 40 trials in the 14-unit T-maze, half of each age group was tested with distributed practice of one trial per day, and the other half was given moderately massed practice of four trials per day, with 10 minutes between trials. The results of this experiment are shown in Figure 2.5. The second order interaction of Age × Practice Condition × Series (blocks of four trials) is statistically significant ($F_{(9,540)} = 5.50$, $p < 0.001$).

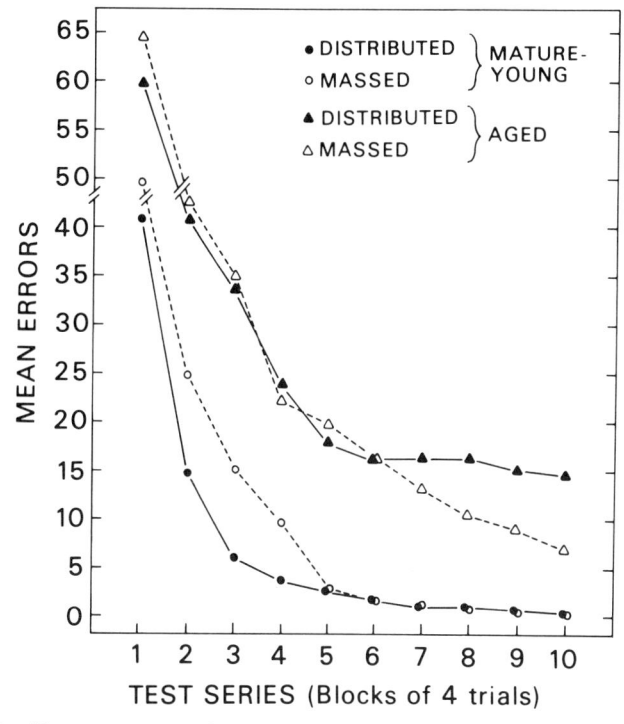

Figure 2.5. Mean errors as a function of age, practice condition, and series (blocks of four trials).

This interaction occurred because mature-young rats reduced errors more quickly under the condition of distributed practice than massed practice, while the aged rats reached a lower level of errors under the condition of massed practice than distributed practice. Also, significant differences as a function of practice condition occurred early in training for mature-young rats (Figure 2.5, series 2, 3, and 4), but occurred late in training for aged rats (Figure 2.5, series 8, 9, and 10). An analysis was made of the number of repetitive or perseverative errors of mature-young and aged rats during early (trials 1–20) and late (trials 21–40) stages of learning. Perseverative errors were defined as six or more consecutive errors at the same cul-de-sac. Table 2.3 gives the mean number of culs-de-sac where six or more errors were obtained, the mean number of culs-de-sac where perseverative responses were obtained, and the mean percentage of perseverative responses. Although the probability of obtaining six consecutive errors

Table 2.3. Analysis of Errors as a Function of Practice Condition and Age.*

		TRIALS 1–20			TRIALS 21–40		
AGE	PRACTICE CONDITION	(A)	(B)	(C)	(A)	(B)	(C)
Young	Distributed	5.4	0.9	14.3	0.4	0.0	0.0
	Massed	6.5	1.4	19.8	0.4	0.0	0.0
Aged	Distributed	7.1	3.8	50.5	3.8	2.5	64.9
	Massed	6.9	3.4	49.1	2.9	1.3	34.2

NOTE: (a) = mean number of culs-de-sac where six or more errors occurred; (b) = mean number of perseverative errors; (c) = mean percentage of perseverative errors.
* Goodrick, 1973a.

in a two-choice situation is 0.014, this probability may be slightly greater for the aged groups than for the mature-young groups because of higher error scores at all choice points. This factor is offset because the perseverative error sequences of the aged rats were normally greater than the minimum of six consecutive errors. Mature-young rats had a significantly lower percentage of perseverative responses than aged rats and the aged distributed practice groups had a significantly higher percentage of perseverative errors than the aged massed practice groups. Although the group percentage differences were not statistically significant on trials 1–20, group differences were highly significant for trials 21–40.

> Also, for the massed practice group, errors were plotted for choice points which were perseverative during early trials, but not during late trials (see Table 2.4). In Table 2.4, series A shows errors made during the first perserverative series of four trials for 33 culs-de-sac. For Series A, errors were made on every trial because perseverative errors are defined in terms of consecutive errors at specific culs-de-sac. Series B represents the first series in which less than four errors were made following at least six consecutive errors. These error plots indicated that errors were made more frequently on the initial trials of a daily series, rather than randomly over the daily series (Goodrick, 1973a, pp. 346–347).

These results are consistent with the earlier studies of this series. Aged rats made more errors than young rats, but aged rats learned

Problem Solving and Age 21

Table 2.4. Errors at 33 Perseverative Choice Points as a Function of Series and Trials for Aged Rats Given Massed Practice.*

	SERIES						
TRIAL	A	B	C	D	E	F	G
1	33	31	25	18	7	5	0
2	33	23	13	10	5	1	0
3	33	17	12	5	0	1	0
4	33	5	4	2	0	0	0
Total perseverative choice points	33	33	26	21	8	5	0

* Goodrick, 1973a.

more efficiently under the conditions of massed practice than under the condition of distributed practice. These results were interpreted as the consequence of short-term memory deficit for the senescent groups. The effects of massed practice were to facilitate error reduction by having repeated trials closely spaced in time. However, this procedure may not work for the aged rat used in the shock-avoidance tests because shocks closely contiguous in time may be extremely disruptive behaviorally.

A second experiment, (Goodrick, 1973a), used slow-learning aged rats which failed to reach a criterion of four errors or fewer on trials 17–20 (distributed practice, one trial per day). Each rat was matched on the basis of errors on trials 17–20 with two other rats. Three matched groups of rats then continued training with either one trial per day, four trials per day, or 12 trials per day. The results are shown in Figure 2.6. The more highly massed practice condition resulted in the fastest, most efficient learning, while distributed practice resulted in persistently high error scores.

This study clearly demonstrated an improvement in learning capability of aged slow-learning rats through the use of massed practice. Aged-senescent rats have also been found to make perseverative errors (repetitive errors at specific culs-de-sac) in all of the preceding studies. If this means that aged rats are behaviorally more rigid than mature-young rats, then forced correct responses may act to facilitate learning of aged rats to a greater degree than mature-young rats. Goodrick

22 Age, Learning Ability, and Intelligence

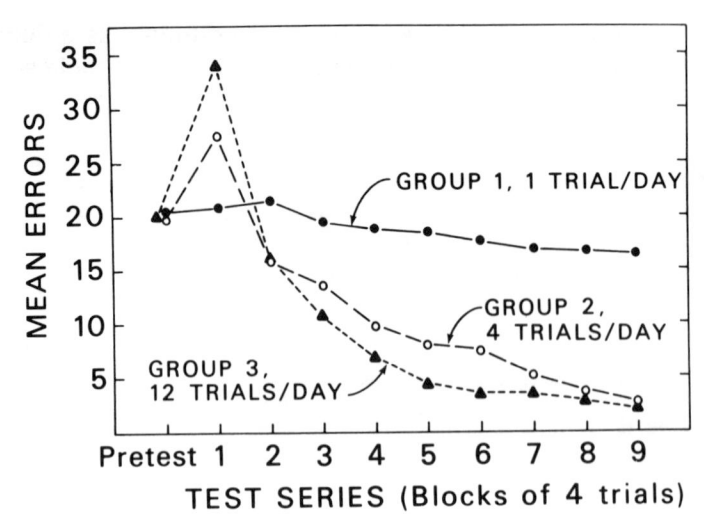

Figure 2.6. Mean errors for slow-learning rats as a function of test series and distribution of practice.

(1975b) specifically tested this hypothesis by training mature-young and aged rats in the 14-unit T-maze with all culs-de-sac blocked. When tested on later trials with the culs-de-sac no longer blocked, the aged rats made fewer errors than the young rats on all 16 trials, although for control rats given 16 training trials, the usual finding of faster learning of mature-young rats than aged rats was obtained (Figure 2.7). This interaction (Age × Training Condition) was highly statistically significant ($F\ (1, 52) = 53.29$, $p < 0.01$). The performance of the aged rats after forced correct response training was at a very high level with very low mean errors and no perseverative responses.

CONCLUSION

The best procedures presently available to study rat age differences in learning or problem-solving ability utilize food rewards and distributed practice in a complex maze-learning procedure. This procedure can provide a clear demonstration of age differences in learning ability and allows the investigator to determine methods of improving the learning ability of slow-learning aged rats.

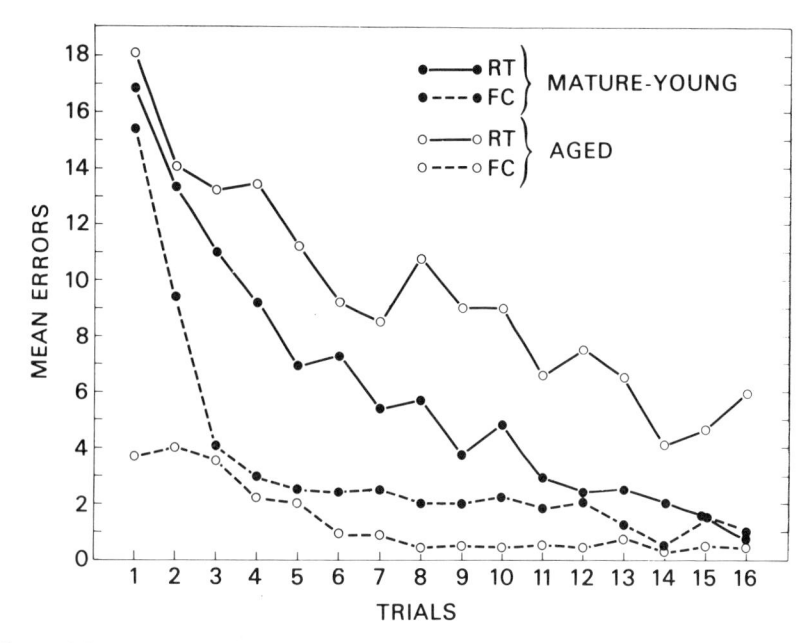

Figure 2.7. Mean errors as a function of age, test condition, and trials. RT = Regular Training and FC = Forced-Correct-Response Training.

REFERENCES

Botwinick, J. *Aging and Behavior.* New York: Springer Publishing Co., Inc., 1973.

Botwinick, J., Brinley, J., and Robbin, J. Learning a position discrimination and position reversals by Sprague-Dawley rats of different ages. *J. Gerontol.* 17:315–319 (1962).

Botwinick, J., Brinley, J., and Robbin, J. Learning and reversing a four-choice multiple Y-maze by rats of three ages. *J. Gerontol.* 18:279–282 (1963).

Doty, B. Age and avoidance conditioning in rats. *J. Gerontol.* 21:287–290 (1966).

Doty, B. Effects of handling on learning of young and aged rats. *J. Gerontol.* 23:142–144 (1968).

Doty, B., and Doty, L. Effects of handling on learning of young and aged rats. *J. Gerontol.* 23:142–144 (1968).

Doty, B., and Doty, L. Effects of handling at various ages on later open-field behaviour. *Can. J. Psychol.* 21:463–470 (1967).

Doty, B., and O'Hare, K. Interaction of shock intensity, age, and handling effects on avoidance conditioning. *Percep. Motor Skills* 23:1311–1314 (1966).

Fields, P. The age factor in multiple-discrimination learning by white rats. *J. Comp. Physiol. Psychol.* **46**:387–389 (1953).

Goodrick, C. Learning, retention, and extinction of a complex maze habit for mature-young and senescent Wistar albino rats. *J. Gerontol.* **23**:298–304 (1968).

Goodrick, C. Variables affecting free exploration responses of male and female Wistar rats as a function of age. *Develop. Psychol.* **4**:440–446 (1971).

Goodrick, C. Learning by mature-young and aged Wistar albino rats as a function of test complexity. *J. Gerontol.* **27**:353–357 (1972).

Goodrick, C. Maze learning of mature-young and aged rats as a function of distribution of practice. *J. Exp. Psychol.* **98**:344–349 (1973a).

Goodrick, C. Error goal-gradients of mature-young and aged rats during training in a 14-unit spatial maze. *Psychol. Rep.* **32**:359–362 (1973b).

Goodrick, C. Behavioral rigidity as a mechanism for facilitation of problem solving for aged rats. *J. Gerontol.* **30**:181–184 (1975a).

Goodrick, C. Behavioral differences in young and aged mice: strain differences for activity measures, operant learning, sensory discrimination, and alcohol preference. *Exp. Aging Res.* **1**:191–207 (1975b).

Jerome, E. Age and learning: experimental results. In J. Birren (ed.), *Handbook of Aging and the Individual*. Chicago: The University of Chicago Press, 1959, pp. 655–699.

Kay, H., and Sime, M. Discrimination learning with old and young rats. *J. Gerontol.* **17**:75–80 (1962).

Kimble, G. *Hilgard and Marquis' Conditioning and Learning*. New York: Appleton-Century-Crofts, 1961.

Munn, N. *Handbook of Psychological Research on the Rat*. Boston: Houghton Mifflin Co., 1950.

Schlettwein-Gesell, D. Survival curves of an old age rat colony. *Gerontologia* **16**:111–115 (1970).

Sime, M., and Kay, H. Inter-problem interference and age. *J. Gerontol.* **17**:81–87 (1962).

Slonaker, J. The normal activity of the rat at different ages. *J. Comp. Neurol. Psych.* **17**:342–359 (1907).

Slonaker, J. Normal activity of the albino rat from birth to natural death, rate of growth, and duration of life. *J. Anim. Behav.* **2**:20–42 (1912).

Sprott, R. L. Passive avoidance conditioning in inbred mice. *J. Comp. Physiol. Psychol.* **80**:327–334 (1972).

Sprott, R. L. The interaction of genotype and environment in the determination of avoidance behavior of aging inbred mice. In D. Bergsma and D. E. Harrison (eds.) *Genetic Effects on Aging*. National Foundation—March of Dimes, Birth Defects Original Article Series. Vol. XIV. New York: Alan R Liss, Inc., 1978, pp. 109–120.

Sprott, R. L., and Stavnes, K. Avoidance learning, behavior genetics, and aging:

a critical review and comments on methodology. *Exp. Aging Res.* **1**:145–168 (1975).

Stone, C. The age factor in animal learning. I. Rats in the problem box and the maze. *Genet. Psychol. Mono.* **5**:1–130 (1929).

Stone, C. The age factor in animal learning. II. Rats on a multiple light discrimination box and a difficult maze. *Genet. Psychol. Mono.* **6**:125–202 (1929).

Verzar-McDougall, E. Studies in learning and memory in ageing rats. *Gerontologia* **1**:65–85 (1957).

Yerkes, R. Modifiability of behavior in its relations to the age and sex of the dancing mouse. *J. Comp. Neurol. Psychol.* **19**:237–271 (1909).

Yerkes, R., and Dodson, J. The relation of strength of stimulus to rapidity of habit formation. *J. Comp. Neurol. Psychol.* **18**:459–482 (1908).

3
Senescence and Learning Behavior in Mice *

Richard L. Sprott

*The Jackson Laboratory
Bar Harbor, Maine*

INTRODUCTION

The previous chapter described the use of rat models for research on a particular set of age-related questions, emphasizing learning ability changes with senescence. The laboratory rat has long been the favorite model for such research because of its short life span (2–3 years) and because of the extensive body of behavioral data collected by psychologists for close to a century. This mass of data provides a baseline of information against which age-related change can be assessed.

The major issues assessed by "rat" gerontologists are the adequacy of the rat as a model for human learning, and the presence or absence of behavioral decrement with advancing age. The first issue (model adequacy) is the most commonly misunderstood. The question is not whether rats are small, dumb versions of humans (they are not!), but rather whether there are basic features common to all mammalian development, which impose an age structure upon behavioral capabilities. Those of us who use animal models assume that commonali-

---
* Preparation of this manuscript was supported by USPHS grant AG 00250 from the National Institute on Aging. The Jackson Laboratory is fully accredited by the American Association for the Accreditation of Laboratory Animal Care.

ties exist. This assumption underlies and affects our research strategies in one of at least two ways. Some investigators, particularly those using rat models, assume process similarity and proceed to ask direct questions about behavioral development. Others, particularly those working with mouse models, use the model to ask questions about the biological nature and extent of commonality. Both groups use behavioral *change* as part of their set of dependent variables, but the types of experiments often differ as a function of the major intended purposes.

The second major issue, behavioral decrement with advancing age, is the subject of this volume. Here the question is not whether behavior changes with advancing age, but why and to what extent. Experiments with animal model systems may not tell us much about the extent of age-dependent human behavior changes, but they may offer important insights into the mechanisms of such changes. For certain classes of behavior, such as activity level and motor coordination, there is no argument about the fact that age-dependent decrements occur (Elias and Elias, 1977; Welford, 1977). For others, for example simple learning tasks for rodents (Jakubczak, 1973) and at least some types of human learning (Baltes and Labouvie, 1977; Schaie, this volume), it is equally clear that decrements do not necessarily occur, at least in healthy individuals. Between these extremes lie the most challenging research areas: those where there is disagreement about whether decrements do or do not usually occur (the questions of extent) and those where decrements are generally acknowledged, but causative mechanisms are obscure (the questions of why).

The laboratory mouse (figure 3.1) is a useful tool for exploring certain types of causative mechanisms primarily because of the genetic definition which exists. Before proceeding with this discussion I should point out that the mouse is not intrinsically a "better" model system than any other comparable mammal (e.g., rats or hamsters), but rather that the mouse has been the standard research organism of mammalian geneticists for more than 50 years. As a consequence, the variety of genotypes and the base of information which has been accumulated for each genotype is vastly greater than for any other nonhuman model.

The advantages of genetic definition will be considered throughout this chapter, so a few definitions may be in order first (see also Green,

28 Age, Learning Ability, and Intelligence

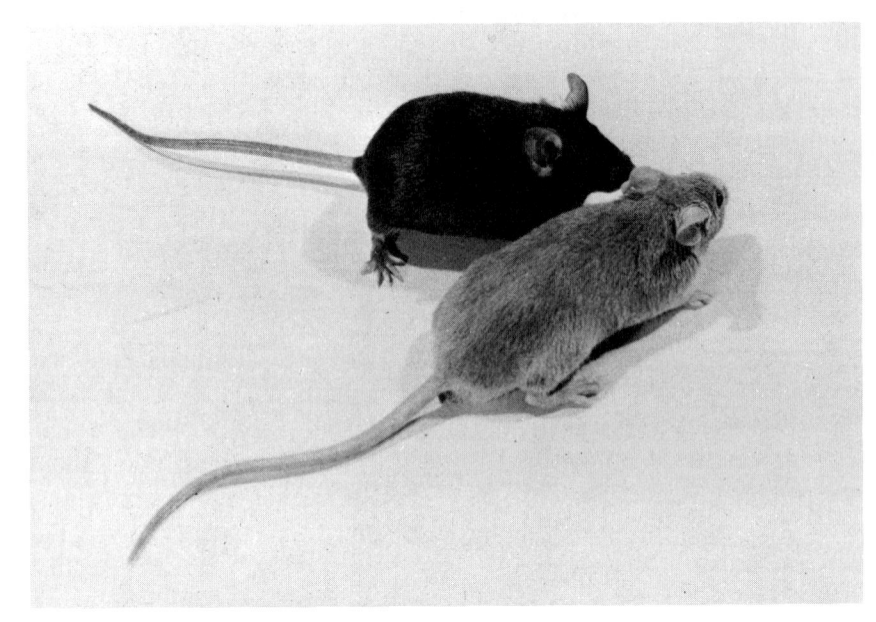

Figure 3.1. Young and old inbred mice. The mouse on the upper left is an 8-week-old male C57BL/6J mouse and the lower mouse in the same picture is a comparable DBA/2J mouse. The mice on the bottom are 3 years of age and are again C57BL/6J (top) and DBA/2J (bottom) males.

1966; Russell and Sprott, 1974). Inbred strains are the product of at least 20 generations of brother-sister mating. The consequence of this mating process is to produce a population of mice as genetically alike as identical twins. Comparisons of the behavior of different inbred strains in the same environment can be used to estimate the importance of genetic variables, while comparisons of the behavior of members of the same strain in different environments can be used to estimate the importance of environmental variables. F_1 hybrid mice, the offspring of a cross between two different inbred strains, are also used frequently in gerontological research. These mice are also genetically uniform; that is, all members of a single generation of a particular cross have the same complement of genes, but they are also heterozygous at all loci where the parental mice had different alleles. One of the consequences of the inbreeding process is the fixation of recessive alleles, which are often deleterious. However, different inbred strains carry different genes at many loci, some dominant, some recessive. When mice of different strains are mated to produce an F_1 hybrid, many of the deleterious recessive alleles of each of the parental types are paired with a nondeleterious allele from the other parental type. As a result, most F_1 hybrid populations are more vigorous and longer-lived than either parent strain.

An additional advantage of using genetically defined populations like inbred strains and F_1 hybrids is their predictable life span and terminal pathology. A wide array of strains is available, with long or short life spans, and with high or low incidences of cancer or susceptibility to other pathological states. It is therefore possible for an investigator to include or exclude particular types of pathology in studies of age-dependent behavior. (Arteriosclerosis, which has not been observed in mice, is an exception.)

LEARNING BEHAVIOR IN AGING MICE

The use of genetically defined mouse models in research on aging is just starting to be undertaken seriously. The studies which have been accomplished so far point to a rapidly evolving research area, which shows signs of fulfilling its utility for research on mechanisms of behavior change. At first it was necessary to collect baseline data on the kinds of behavior which mice could learn and perform for most of their life span. Before 1967 most behavioral research with mice was conducted with 2–3-month-old mice. A few investigators (Meier, 1964) used mice as old as 6 months, but no one knew, or perhaps even worried about, whether 2- and 3-month-old mice were behaviorally mature. This lack of information posed both a problem and an opportunity. The problem is obvious: How can one compare senescent behavior with mature adult behavior, if the latter has not been defined? The opportunity follows directly from the problem. Given that each investigator must determine behavioral maturity for the tasks under study by empirical test, the opportunity exists to develop tasks specific for gerontological research and to apply these tasks in life span research strategies.

The most difficult problem in age-dependent learning research (just as in comparable human studies) is the elimination of extraneous variables. The two approaches most commonly used are to try to design tasks which remove or minimize the unwanted influence (e.g., learning tasks which require little movement to eliminate motor skill) or to assess the degree of influence of the variable and adjust the evaluation of performance to compensate for the extraneous influence (e.g., adjust for influence of the passage of time in test-retest measures). In practice, the two approaches must be used together since it is virtually impossible to eliminate every extraneous influence or to compensate for several at the same time. One result is a preoccupation with method which is apparent in all gerontological research and especially in the animal model research described in this and the preceding chapter.

Since a number of reviews have been published which list behavioral characteristics of mice which might be of interest to gerontologists (Sprott, 1975, 1976; Sprott and Stavnes, 1975; Elias and Elias, 1976; Omenn, 1977), the discussion which follows will focus on experiments which have a direct bearing upon learning ability or its measurement. The discussion is organized so that the influence of extraneous variables is presented first, followed by a discussion of learning ability per se.

Age-dependent decrements in motor coordination skills are so obvious that very few studies have been conducted to describe or to quantify the extent of the decrement. Miquel and Blasco (1978) have described a simple "tightrope" test of motor skill, which is described as "neuromuscular competence," for use with mice. The mouse is forced to grasp a 1 mm string with its forepaws and then must work its way to one end of the string without falling. Four-month-old male C57BL/6J mice perform this task readily, while only 60% of 9.5–14.5-month-old and 20% of 36–37-month-old mice are able to do so. We are currently conducting a large-scale test of motor skill in our laboratory using a rotating lucite rod. The rod is 1.5 inches in diameter, and can be rotated at 1 or 6 revolutions per minute. The mouse's task is to stay on the rod for 90 seconds at either speed. Inability to stay on the rod at the relatively high 6 rpm speed occurs with very moderate motor skill decrements, while inability to stay on the slow 1 rpm rod indicates gross loss of motor skill. While our tests with male C57BL/6J and DBA/2J mice, at ages ranging from 2 to 30 months, are still in progress, it is clear that mice of both genotypes show a great loss in high-speed rotorod ability by 18 months of age. On the slow rod, C57BL/6J mice show some loss by 18 months of age, and DBA/2J mice show considerable loss. Testing on the high-speed rod at 24 and 30 months is not worthwhile since no mouse so far tested has been capable of performing satisfactorily. A few C57BL/6J mice have learned the slow rod task at 30 months.

Similar results in a swimming test have been reported for C57BL/6J mice (Wright, Werboff, and Haggett, 1971) ranging in age from 350 to 845 days. Mice were forced to swim in a constant temperature (23.5°C) water bath until they sank for a period of 5 seconds. The two oldest groups (720 and 845 days) showed significant reductions in the time they were able to swim (Figure 3.2).

What has any of this to do with learning ability? First, there is the obvious point that poor performance in older subjects does not necessarily reflect loss of learning ability as usually understood, but rather may simply reflect loss of the ability to perform the motor aspects of the task. The point does indeed seem ridiculously obvious in this case, but the problem recurs again and again in subtler form throughout the rest of this volume. My personal bias is to look first for this kind of effect when an age decrement is observed, rather than to look first for the losses in brain function assumed to underlie "true" decrements in learning ability. The fact that there is an apparent strain difference in the rate at which a decrement occurs is sometimes used as evidence that aging occurs at different, genetically programmed rates. While

32 Age, Learning Ability, and Intelligence

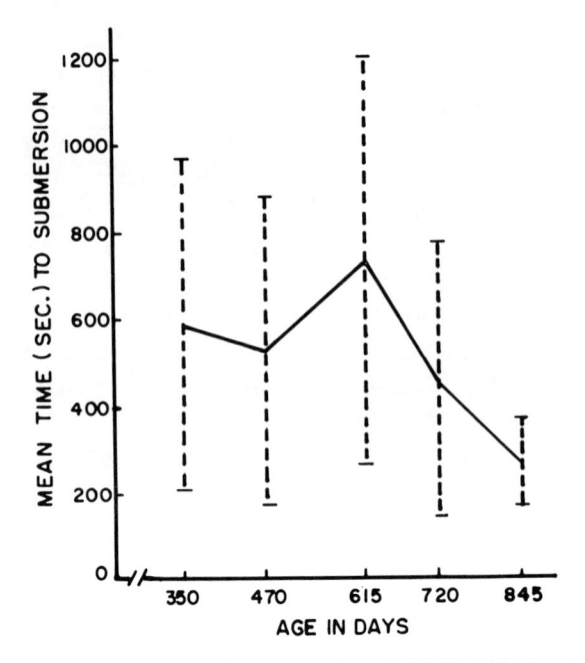

Figure 3.2. Mean time in seconds to submersion of C57BL/6J mice at various ages. Mice in this experiment were required to swim with a tail weight until they reached a point of 5 continuous seconds of submersion. (Reprinted with permission from: Wright, W. E., Werboff, J., and Haggett, B. N. Aging and Water Submersion in C57BL/65 Mice: Initial performance and retest as a function of recovery and water temperature. *Developmental Psychobiology,* **4:** 363–373, 1971.)

this may in fact be the case, it is also possible, as is likely in the present example, that the baseline skill levels are different. A difference in baseline skill level, coupled with differential susceptibilities to a spectrum of pathological conditions, could produce apparent differences in aging rate, where no real differences exist. The question of health status is also an important issue which will be discussed later in this chapter and in the following one. In any case, there is little argument that motor skills decline in aging mice and men. It is therefore necessary to account for or to eliminate motor skill decrements in learning ability tests, if our interest is in ability rather than performance.

Age-dependent activity levels are typically measured in the open-field or in running wheels and decrements are usually observed in older animals. Since an age-dependent decline in activity level is an ubiquitous finding, it is intriguing that much more attention has been given to studies of activity level than to the motor skill decrements. Decrements in activity level could simply be a reflection of the same muscle changes which obviously are a part of declining motor skill. Shephard (1978), in a discussion of the effects of exercise on human longevity, points out that while activity levels of various human subgroups differ greatly, muscle deterioration is relatively constant. Some other factor must be influencing activity level, and motivation is usually assumed to be the key to the differences. Motivational differences are relatively easy to find in some human comparisons: high interest in the case of athletes, necessity in primitive societies, and lack of time or interest in practitioners of sedentary occupations. Similar examples can also be created in mouse model systems by manipulation of access to food, or by providing strong negative stimuli to be avoided. If all motivational differences were this obvious, research on aging would be far simpler, and few investigators would have much interest in activity level. However, there are some differences in human activity level not explained by necessity or muscle change in which all groups show some decline. Shephard postulates that the "universal decline" may be under the control of a hypothalamic activity center for "habitual activity," which is adjusted downward with advancing age. A center of this type could be specific for activity, or it could have much broader effects upon a variety of behaviors with a motivational component.

Since the activity levels which are measured in the open-field and the running wheel are usually levels of voluntary activity, it is assumed that motivation plays a major determining role. Virtually all such studies in mice show lower activity levels in older (from 12 to 30 months) subjects in activity wheels (Goodrick, 1975; Wax, 1977), in the open-field (Sprott and Eleftheriou, 1974; Goodrick, 1975), in a circular runway (Goodrick, 1967), and in photocell measurement of cage activity (Abel, 1978). While activity levels decline in all of these experiments, the magnitude of the decline is dependent upon both the genotype of the mouse (Sprott and Eleftheriou, 1974; Goodrick, 1975) and upon the environment in which the mice were housed and tested (Sprott and Eleftheriou, 1974). C57BL/6J mice have higher activity levels when young than do DBA/2J or A/J mice and show much greater reductions as they age (a situation which probably parallels the performance of aging athletes). Abel (1978) also showed that the activity level of older (12–13 months) C57BL/6J mice was more depressed by ethanol or pentobarbital injection than that of young (2–3 months) C57BL/6J mice.

While it is obvious that levels of voluntary activity decline with advancing age, we do not know whether this is true of other voluntary behaviors such as grooming, social interaction, or aggression. Nor do we know the degree to which the age decrement can be manipulated by practice or environmental factors. Goodrick (1974) has shown that exercise in activity wheels at 23 months of age resulted in higher levels of open-field activity in F_2 mice descended from A/J and C57BL/6J parental strains. Sprott and Eleftheriou observed large differences in the activity levels of older (18–30 months), but not younger (2–6 months) mice of the same strains (C57BL/6J and DBA/2J), when they were housed and tested in separate laboratories.

The final major set of variables to be considered before looking at learning ability are the stimulus sensitivity variables. Obviously an animal can only learn a task if it can perceive the appropriate stimuli and conduct the appropriate information to its central nervous system. In a simple test of reflex integrity (Sprott and Symons, 1976), a mild electrical stimulus to the palate of DBA/2J and C57BL/6J mice aged 2, 8, 20, 25, and 30 months revealed no age decrement in this function. On the other hand, Goodrick (1975) has shown decrements in task discrimination ability in male 23-month-old C57BL/6J and A/J mice and (1967) in 26-month-old female C57BL/6J mice. Recent results reported by Henry (1979) are the most startling yet reported. Henry administered a variety of tests of auditory function to C57BL/6J and CBA/J mice and found that C57BL/6J mice began to show hearing loss at 200 days of age, while CBA mice did not show auditory loss until well beyond the age of the strain's mean life span. The integrity of the visual system in aging mice has not yet been reported.

A very distinct advantage of the use of animal models is the opportunity to observe behavioral development for the entire life span, and for a single experimenter, or a generation of experimenters, to observe many life span cycles. The earliest studies of the relationships between advancing age and learning ability assumed that mice were "old" at 12 to 15 months of age (e.g., Oliverio and Bovet, 1966; Freund and Walker, 1971). At the time this assumption did not seem unreasonable, since then reported life spans of male C57BL/6J mice (used by Freund and Walker) and DBA/2J mice (used by Oliverio and Bovet) have risen from 539 days and 415 days respectively (Russell, 1966) in 1956 to 888 days and 660 days (Les, 1969) respectively. Improved husbandry and the elimination of certain pathogens from breeding and maintenance colonies appear to be the major factors in this increased longevity (Myers, 1978). It is therefore not surprising that these studies did not show evidence of a decrement in learning ability in "old" mice in a shuttle box avoidance task (Freund and Walker, 1971) or in maze learning or shuttle box learning (Oliverio and Bovet, 1966) that cannot be accounted for as either a maturation effect or simply the result of the passage of time.

Maturation effects, such as a brief performance peak at 60 days of age in the Oliverio and Bovet study described above, performance dips around the same age in water maze learning (Meier and Foshee, 1963; Meier, 1964), and strain reversals in relative performance in passive-avoidance learning (Sprott, 1972) and active avoidance (Buckholtz, 1974; Stavnes and Sprott, 1975), are observed frequently. No adequate test of life span behavior can ignore the possibility of the presence of maturation effects. In practice this means that a simple cross-sectional study, which tests mice (and no doubt people as well) at two or three ages, is quite likely to be misleading. Unfortunately, few investigators have the time and resources to test significant numbers of subjects at more than two or three ages.

In studies of learning behavior which used mice that were old enough to be senescent (26–30 months) results which appear to be contradictory have been obtained. Goodrick (1967) has shown a decrement in water maze learning in 26-month-old female C57BL/6J mice, compared to comparable 4-month-old mice. Goodrick (1975) has also shown a decrement in the extinction of a learned operant task, but not in its acquisition, in 26-month-old female C57BL/6J mice and in 23-month-old male and female A/J mice. In studies of passive-avoidance learning in this laboratory (Sprott, 1978) no evidence of a senescent decrement was observed in healthy male C57BL/6J and DBA/2J mice at ages ranging up to 30 months, while some slight evidence of a decrement was observed in 30-month-old C57BL/6J × DBA/2J F_1 hybrid mice (Figure 3.3).

An argument is often made (see the previous chapter) that tasks such as passive-avoidance learning, which minimize the effects of the

36 Age, Learning Ability, and Intelligence

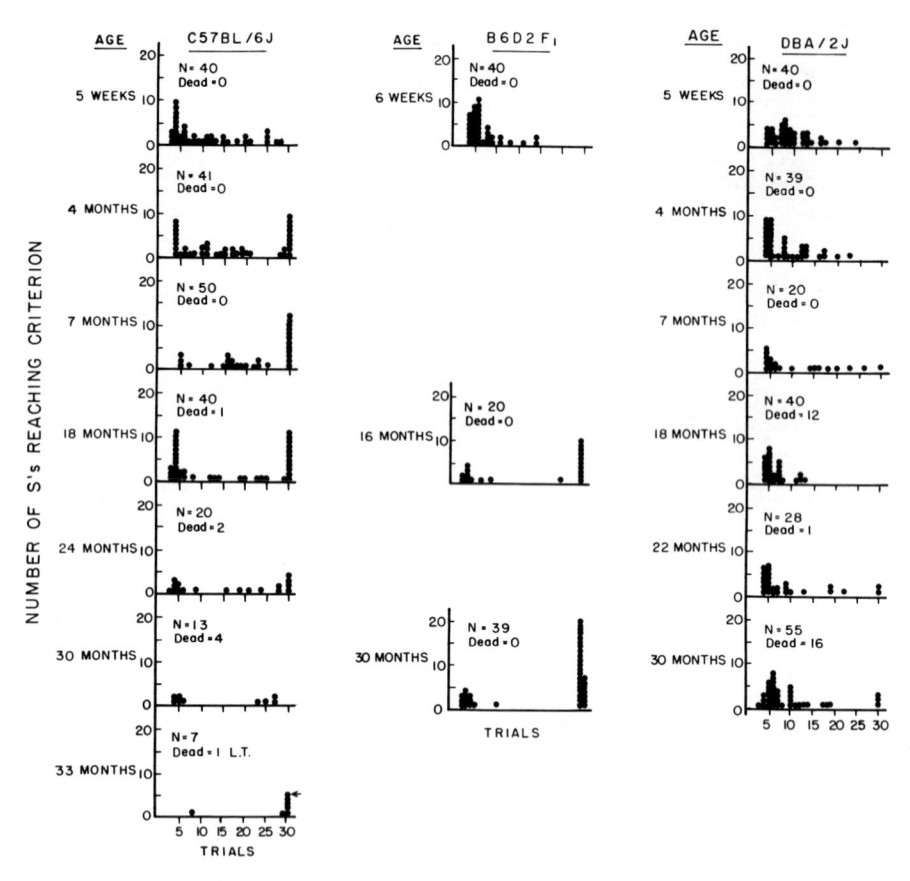

Figure 3.3 Distributions of the performance of inbred mice in a passive-avoidance situation at ages ranging from 5 weeks to 33 months. Mice were required to stay on a 1 inch × 6 inch shelf to avoid foot-shock. Each dot represents a single subject which reached a criterion of 3 successive successful avoidances. The mice were given 1 trial each day to a maximum of 30 trials. Maturation effects are indicated by differences in the performance of 5-week-old and 4-month-old mice. The poor performance of 30-month-old F_1 hybrid mice suggests a senescent effect in the hybrid genotype. Parental genotype mice were more susceptible to death as a result of the "stress" in the testing situation.

motor skill and activity variables are not of sufficient complexity to evoke learning ability decrements even if they exist. In one sense the argument cannot be denied. It can only be disproven by demonstrating learning ability decrements in more complex tasks which are not contaminated by other variables, perhaps an impossible feat. In any case, the argument is probably specious. A demonstration that a particular type of learning ability is intact for the entire life span of a subject population can only mean that learning ability *of that particular type* is not affected by senescence. It does not mean that *all* learning abilities follow the same pattern, nor are such results usually employed to bolster such a position. Some learning abilities in mice and men are preserved for a lifetime in healthy individuals, others may decline gradually, and still others may decline precipitously in the terminal phase of life. What is important is to discover which kinds of ability follow particular patterns in order to determine the relative vulnerability of the many abilities which make up a behavioral repertoire. Finally, it should be obvious that studies in which learning abilities remain intact for the life span of the subjects clearly demonstrate that it is possible to eliminate the influence of extraneous variables known to change with advancing age.

Another, more serious, challenge to studies such as these just described can be made. It can be argued that none of these experiments assess behaviors significant to the function and survival of the test population. There is at least some validity to this point of view. The only defense we can presently muster is that we cannot hope to understand changes we observe in complex behaviors before we have an understanding of the simpler behaviors, which are likely to be their component parts.

CONCLUSIONS

Genetically defined mice have not yet been used to full advantage. Almost all experiments have included one, or perhaps two, inbred strains, tested at two or three ages. While effects of genetic variables upon the age course of sensory ability, motor skill, and activity level have been observed, none have been reported for learning ability. Although it is possible that aging patterns of learning ability are similar in all mice, too few tests have been conducted so far for a meaningful assessment. A basic core of information has been assembled on the learning abilities of a few strains of mice. Better use of this resource should now become a high-priority research objective. Experimental designs which test more complex learning abilities, without confounding by extraneous variables, should be assessed not on the members of a single inbred strain or a single heterozygous population, but rather should be applied to a meaningful array of genotypes, for example, two inbred strains and the F_1 hybrid resulting from their cross. (See Russell and Sprott, 1974, for a fuller discussion of genetic strategies.)

A comparison of the behavior reported here for mice and that in the previous chapter for rats shows considerable similarity. The similarity is in part a function of the similarity in techniques and hypotheses being tested, but it is also strong evidence for the existence of some generality across species in behavioral age patterns. Cutler (1978) has pointed out a number of strong similarities in the senescence of many mammalian species. It is therefore not wholly unreasonable to assume that some of the processes we observe in more than one rodent species have counterparts in primate species including man. At the very least, the arguments about the presence of age decrements in learning ability and their putative causes are very similar, as subsequent chapters in this volume will show.

REFERENCES

Abel, E. L. Effects of ethanol and pentobarbital in mice of different ages. *Physiol. Psychol.* **6**:366–368 (1978).

Baltes, P. B., and Labouvie, G. V. Adult development of intellectual performance: description, explanation, and modification. In C. Eisdorfer and M. P. Lawton (eds.), *The Psychology of Adult Development and Aging*. Washington, D.C.: American Psychological Association, 1977, pp. 157–219.

Buckholtz, N. S. Shuttle-avoidance learning of mice: effects of post-trial pentylenetetrazol, strain, and age. *Psych. Rep.* **35**:319–326 (1974).

Cutler, R. G. Evolutionary biology of senescence. In J. A. Behnke, C. E. Finch, and G. B. Moment (eds.), *The Biology of Aging*. New York: Plenum Press, 1978, pp. 311–360.

Elias, M. F., and Elias, P. K. Motivation and activity. In J. E. Birren and K. W. Schaie (eds.), *Handbook of the Psychology of Aging*. New York: Van Nostrand Reinhold Co., 1977, pp. 357–383.

Elias, P. K., and Elias, M. F. Effects of age on learning ability: contributions from the animal literature. *Exp. Aging Res.* **2**:165–186 (1976).

Freund, G., and Walker, D. W. The effect of aging on acquisition and retention of shuttle box avoidance in mice. *Life Sci.* **10**:1343–1349 (1971).

Goodrick, C. L. Behavioral characteristics of young and senescent inbred female mice of the C57BL/6J strain. *J. Gerontol.* **22**:459–464 (1967).

Goodrick, C. L. The effects of exercise on longevity and behavior of hybrid mice which differ in coat color. *J. Gerontol.* **29**:129–133 (1974).

Goodrick, C. L. Behavioral differences in young and aged mice: strain differences for activity measures, operant learning, sensory discrimination, and alcohol preference. *Exp. Aging Res.* **1**:191–207 (1975).

Goodrick, C. L. Effect of voluntary wheel exercise on food intake, water intake, and body weight for C57BL/6J mice and mutations which differ in maximal body weight. *Physiol. Behav.* **21**:345–351 (1978).

Green, E. L. Breeding systems. In E. L. Green (ed.), *Biology of the Laboratory Mouse*. 2nd Edition. New York: McGraw-Hill Book Co., 1966, pp. 11–22.

Henry, K. R. Strain differences in behavioral and physiological expressions of age-related hearing loss in the laboratory mouse. Paper presented at Annual Meeting of Behav. Genet. Assoc., Middletown, Conn. (1979).

Jakubczak, L. E. Age and animal behavior. In C. E. Eisdorfer and M. P. Lawton (eds.), *The Psychology of Adult Development and Aging*. Washington, D.C.: American Psychological Association, 1973, pp. 98–111.

Les, E. P. (Abstract) Paper presented at 20th Annual Meeting of the Amer. Assoc. for Lab. Sci. Joliet, Il.: AALAS, Pub. No. 69–2 (1969).

Meier, G. W. Differences in maze performances as a function of age and strain of house mice. *J. Comp. Physiol. Psychol.* **589**:418–422 (1964).

Meier, G. W., and Foshee, D. P. Genetics, age, and the variability of learning performances *J. Genet. Psychol.* **102**:267–275 (1963).

Miquel, J., and Blasco, M. A simple technique for evaluation of vitality loss in aging mice, by testing their muscular coordination and vigor. *Exp. Gerontol.* **13**:389–396 (1978).

Myers, D. D. Review of disease patterns and lifespan in aging mice: genetic and environmental interactions. In D. Bergsma and D. E. Harrison (eds.), *Genetic Effects on Aging*. National Foundation—March of Dimes, Birth Defects Original Article Series. Vol. XIV. New York: Alan R. Liss, Inc., 1978, pp. 41–53.

Oliverio, A., and Bovet, D. Effects of age on maze learning and avoidance conditioning of mice. *Life Sci.* **5**:1317–1324 (1966).

Omenn, G. S. Behavior genetics. In J. E. Birren and K. W. Schaie (eds.), *Handbook of the Psychology of Aging*. New York: Van Nostrand Reinhold Co., 1977, pp. 190–218.

Russell, E. S. Lifespan and aging patterns. In E. L. Green (ed.), *The Biology of the Laboratory Mouse*. 2nd Edition. New York: McGraw-Hill Book Co., 1966, pp. 511–519.

Russell, E. S., and Sprott, R. L. Genetics and the aging nervous system. In G. J. Maletta (ed.), *Survey Report on the Aging Nervous System*. USPHS

Publ. No. 74–296. Washington, D. C.: U.S. Government Printing Office, 1974.

Shephard, R. J. Exercise and aging. In J. A. Behnke, C. E. Finch, and G. B. Moment (eds.), *The Biology of Aging*. New York: Plenum Press, 1978, pp. 131–149.

Sprott, R. L. Passive avoidance conditioning in inbred mice: effects of shock intensity, age, and genotype. *J. Comp. Physiol. Psychol.* **80**:327–334 (1972).

Sprott, R. L. Behavioral characteristics of C57BL/6J, DBA/2J, and B6D2F$_1$ mice which are potentially useful for gerontological research. *Exp. Aging Res.* **1**:313–323 (1975).

Sprott, R. L. Behavior genetics in aging rodents. In M. F. Elias, B. E. Eleftheriou, and P. K. Elias (eds.), *Special Review of Experimental Aging Review*. Bar Harbor: *Exp. Aging Res.*, 1976, pp. 19–29.

Sprott, R. L. The interaction of genotype and environment in the determination of avoidance behavior of aging inbred mice. In D. Bergsma and D. E. Harrison (eds.), *Genetic Effects on Aging*. National Foundation—March of Dimes, Birth Defects Original Article Series. Vol. XIV. New York: Alan R. Liss, Inc., 1978, pp. 109–120.

Sprott, R. L., and Eleftheriou, B. E. Open-field behavior in aging inbred mice. *Gerontologia* **20**:155–162 (1974).

Sprott, R. L., and Stavnes, K. Avoidance learning, behavior genetics, and aging: a critical review and comment on methodology. *Exp. Aging Res.* **1**:145–168 (1975).

Sprott, R. L., and Symons, J. P. The effects of age and genotype upon the jaw-jerk reflex in inbred mice. *J. Gerontol.* **31**:660–662 (1976).

Stavnes, K., and Sprott, R. L. Effects of age and genotype on acquisition of an active avoidance response in mice. *Develop. Psychobiol.* **8**:437–445 (1975).

Wax, T. M. Effects of age, strain, and illumination intensity on activity and self-selection of light-dark schedules in mice. *J. Comp. Physiol. Psychol.* **91**:51–62 (1977).

Welford, A. T. Motor performance. In J. E. Birren and K. W. Schaie (eds.), *Handbook of the Psychology of Aging*. New York: Van Nostrand Reinhold Co., 1977, pp. 450–496.

Wright, W. E., Werboff, J., and Haggett, B. N. Aging and water submersion in C57BL/6J mice: initial performance and retest as a function of recovery and water temperature. *Develop. Psychobiol.* **4**:363–373 (1971).

4
Age Changes in Intelligence *

K. Warner Schaie

*Andrus Gerontology Center
and
Department of Psychology
University of Southern California
Los Angeles, California*

INTRODUCTION

It has long been thought that intellectual powers peak in early adulthood and then show an inexorable decline. This thinking has been based upon public stereotypes about the elderly, perhaps with the implicit assumption that there ought to be isomorphism between decline of physical vigor and intellectual abilities. Some of the earlier psychological research literature, based primarily on cross-sectional data, seemed to support the stereotype. Nevertheless, there has always been a discordant note, because folk myth also tells us that wisdom comes with age and that the elderly are a repository of those values which provide societal stability and quality of life. Recent theoretical analyses (Flavell, 1970; Schaie, 1977/78) moreover suggest that while there may be isomorphism between biological structure and psychological function in childhood, such isomorphism ceases when

---
* This chapter represents an integration and summary of material, parts of which have been previously discussed elsewhere. Expanded versions of parts of this chapter may be found in Schaie (1977/78, 1978, 1979a, 1979b) and Schaie and Schaie (1979).

maturity is reached. Data from longitudinal studies and from replications of cross-sectional work have further questioned what we thought we knew about adult intelligence. In fact there has been much recent controversy regarding the "myth" of intellectual decline (Baltes and Schaie, 1974; Schaie, 1974; Horn and Donaldson, 1976) as well as what has become a "myth" about the "myth" (Botwinick, 1977; Baltes and Schaie, 1976; Horn and Donaldson, 1977; Schaie and Baltes, 1977).

In this chapter I will try to sketch the problem as succinctly as possible, but the reader should be warned to begin with, that although I will attempt to present a balanced view, it will primarily be an account of my own position. That is what I was commissioned to do, and that is what this chapter is all about.

I will begin with a historical review of the study of adult intelligence and will then deal with certain theoretical and methodological issues which cannot be overlooked if one is to understand this topic. In this context I will need to talk about models or meta-models for the description of changes in adult intelligence, the nature of the alternate data bases upon which our knowledge is built, and the issue of construct validity of findings across ages and cohorts. I will then give a brief summary of findings on age changes for the commonly used Wechsler test, and a more detailed summary of our findings with the Primary Mental Abilities Test. The latter will be qualified by what we have learned about the impact of health and environmental factors on maintenance or decline of intellectual functions. I will then summarize what I think to be the current status of the question of intellectual decline with age, and finally will comment on the problem of studying intelligence in the old with tests developed for the young.

Why Study Intelligence in Adulthood?

Early empirical work on intelligence was directed toward investigating the acquisition of functions and skills in early life. But theoretical writers such as G. Stanley Hall (1922), H. L. Hollingworth (1927), and Sydney Pressey (1939) soon awakened interest in some of the complexities related to attainment of peak performance level, transformations of intellectual structure, and decremental changes occurring in late middle age and in the elderly.

An early finding of interest to students of intellectual development came from Yerkes' (1921) study of World War I soldiers. He reported that the apparent level of mental function for young adults was only at about 13 years of age. Terman's original standardization of the Binet Intelligence Test for American use also assumed that intellectual development peaked at age 16 and then remained constant (Terman, 1916). Such assumptions were soon questioned, however, by data from other empirical work. Jones and Conrad (1933), for example, on the basis of cross-sectional studies in a New England community, showed substantial age differences across adulthood on some but little differences on other subtests on the Army Alpha Test.

Similar findings were obtained in the standardization studies connected with the development of the Wechsler-Bellevue Intelligence Test. This work emphasized the fact that growth of intelligence does not end in early adolescence, that peak ages are not the same for different aspects of intellectual functioning, and that age differences are not uniform across the full spectrum of abilities tapped by most of the major batteries measuring intellectual development (Wechsler, 1939).

All these matters would be of historical interest only, if it were not for the fact that omnibus measures of intelligence are quite useful in predicting a person's competence in dealing with our society's educational system and in succeeding in vocational pursuits which require educationally based knowledge and skills. Certain ability measures have also had some use in predicting competence in meeting specific situational demands. And the analysis of patterns of intellectual performance has been found helpful by clinicians in the diagnostic appraisal of psychopathology. In work with the elderly, moreover, it is apparent that some determination of intellectual competence may be directly relevant to such issues as mandatory retirement, educability for new careers and life roles, maintenance of individual living arrangements, and the conservation and disposition of property (Matarrazo, 1972; Schaie and Schaie, 1979; Schaie and Willis, 1978).

If we are to address the above issues intelligently, we must then know the developmental patterns of different aspects of mental ability and the ages at which developmental peaks occur. We can then differentiate age from cohort differences, can distinguish between obsolescence and decrement, and will perhaps be able to understand what variables contribute to the apparent fact that some individuals show intellectual decrement beginning with early adulthood while others maintain and increase their functioning until advanced old age.

Intelligence and Competence: A Brief Historical Contemplation

Measures of intellectual functioning, of course, are useful only inasmuch as they can help us predict criteria of social consequence. Indeed, the beginning of the mental test movement almost aborted when Wissler's (1901) classical study showed that the kind of measures of ability suggested by the early work of Galton (1883) and J. McK. Cattell (1890) showed only trivial correlations with measures of social consequence such as success in formal educational situations. The successful takeoff of intelligence testing began when Binet and Simon (1908) showed that objective measures of intellectual ability could be applied to the useful task of screening for uneducable children in public schools. Paradoxically, the earlier unsuccessful attempts were indeed proper ways of measuring intelligence as a set of multiple unitary traits, while the latter presented us with a combination of such traits which tended to assess situation-specific competence. But before we go any further let us attempt to distinguish properly between the concepts of intelligence and competence.

In the introduction to their monograph, Connolly and Bruner (1974) suggest that the term competence refers to intelligence in its broadest sense, that is, in its aspect of *"knowing how* rather than simply *knowing that* (authors' italics)." They distinguish between a narrow definition of intelligence as a passive structure of intellect à la Guilford (1967), whether inherited or acquired, and a much broader delineation of competence as a construct implying action which may change the environment as well as adapt to the environment. Three attributes of competence are said to be the ability to select features from the total environment that are required information for initiating a course of action, to initiate a sequence of movements designed to achieve the planned objectives, and to learn from successes and failures in order to formulate new plans.

It follows then that competent behavior will involve the application of the structure of intellect in specific situations, the attributes of which may well interact with the developmental level of the individual under study. When discussing intelligence we must, of course, distinguish between the observed or phenotypic measures of a particular construct, and the latent trait or genotypic construct in itself. This means that phenotypic measures of unitary traits of intelligence, as represented by the more commonly used intelligence tests, ought to be situation-specific with respect to competence, even though within a given level of ontogeny they might be generalizable across different situations with respect to the intellectual process utilized. A measure of intellectual ability which assesses a single trait, no matter how elegant, will not suffice fully to assess the expression of competence in a given situation. Hence, optimal combinations of unitary traits will always be required to elicit competent behavior within as well as across situations (Schaie, 1978).

The intelligence-competence distinction may be summarized by proposing that competence be viewed as the phenotypic expression of a particular combination of genotypic intelligence factors which, given minimally required levels of motivational incentives, will permit adaptive behavior within a specific situation or class of situations. Intelligence, on the other hand, would be viewed as that spectrum of genotypic factors which might be abstracted from phenotypic expressions of adaptive behavior measured *across* situations.

Given the above distinction, it appears that we have been shifting back and forth historically from a competence model to an intelligence model. Which is to be preferred obviously depends upon one's predilection for construct purity and elegance (the intelligence side) or for application to practical assessment issues (the competence side). But different theoretical models and data bases will also have much influence upon the direction chosen. We will next proceed to examine the latter issues.

THEORETICAL AND METHODOLOGICAL ISSUES

In this section we will first consider models of intelligence and then examine the different data bases which are available or needed for the investigation of adult intelligence. Attention will also be given briefly to the problem of the generalizability of construct validity across cohorts and ages.

Models of Intelligence

The discussion of intellectual development ought to begin by specifying the nature of the construct whose development is to be understood. We have already distinguished between the concepts of intelligence and competence. It will now be helpful to engage in a brief historical analysis of different models of intelligence to see whether and how this distinction has been operationalized. Four basic approaches will be considered: (1) the notion of intelligence as a general construct, (2) multifactor theories of intelligence, (3) the distinction of fluid and crystallized intelligence, and (4) stage theories about adult intellectual development.

Intelligence as a general construct. Spearman (1927) believed that all intellectual activities contained something of a common element which he labeled the "g" factor. He observed that when one studies the intercorrelations among test items one can find high agreement among items which appear to be measures of intellectual functions. Omnibus tests of intelligence (such as the Binet test and its successors) have tended to be quite successful in predicting performance in certain educational situations. A variety of "g" factors might be found, however, if one were to examine test items predictive of performance in noneducational situations or, for that matter, in nontraditional educational situations.

Multifactor theories of intelligence. Tests designed to measure a number of factors related to intelligence include test items which have variance on significant aspects of intellectual performance as well as general factors. Resulting test batteries (the Wechsler tests are a prominent example) have only moderate correlations between their parts, although their sum (as expressed in a total IQ) will measure competence for situations for which the particular component parts are important.

Thurstone (1938) studied the correlations among approximately 60 different measures of intelligence and concluded that one can identify a number of factors which have little or no relationship with one another. Thurstone's factors (as well as the structure-of-intellect model of Guilford, 1967) represent latent variables which can be measured only indirectly. These factors may indeed be the building blocks of intelligence, but, paradoxically, knowledge of an individual's standing on any one of them will not help predict competence in a specific situation or across classes of situations, except in the unusual case where a single factor accounts for most of the reliable variance in an observance behavior. Although it is not likely that new factors accounting for much variance will appear late in life, it is still possible that some intellectual abilities may account for much variance early in life.

Fluid and crystallized intelligence. Abilities which depend most on sociocultural influences form one class, called the *crystallized* abilities. Examples of this class would be number facility, verbal comprehension and general information. Other abilities may be quite independent of acculturation, and their function may depend more on genetic endowment, the neurophysiological state of the individual and perhaps on incidental learning. These latter abilities are called *fluid* and are represented by such variables as memory span, inductive reasoning and figural relations (cf. Cattell, 1963). The contention that crystallized abilities reach an early adult optimal level and remain stable from then on while the fluid abilities show early decline (Horn, 1970) has recently been subjected to serious challenge (Plemons, Willis, and Baltes, 1978).

Stage theories of adult development. The Genevan model of intelligence (Flavell, 1963) places emphasis on the development of biologically based cognitive structures which produce qualitative changes in the way cognitive operations are conducted as the individual matures. By the time adulthood is reached, the final stage of formal operations should have been attained and should be maintained from then on (Flavell, 1970). However, Piaget (1972) has recently suggested that not all adults attain the stage of formal operations, and that formal operations are not applied uniformly to all substantive areas of cognitive behavior (see also Schaie and Marquette, 1975).

A recent extension (Schaie, 1977/78) considers the possibility of three adult stages: an *achieving* stage during which the young adult strives towards goal orientation and role independence, a *responsible* stage involving long-term goal integration and increased problem-solving skills, and a *reintegrative* stage during which there is relinquishment of occupational and familial responsibilities accompanied by the simplification of cognitive structures through selective attention to meaningful environmental demands. This conceptualization is quite compatible with stage theories of adult moral development (Kohlberg, 1973), of ego development (Erikson, 1964), and with Havighurst's (1972, 1979) developmental task approach.

Data Bases for the Study of Adult Intelligence

A better understanding of the research literature on intellectual development as well as the recent controversies sparked by this literature will require brief consideration of: (1) the differentiation of age changes and age differences which is so important in understanding the discrepancies of findings from cross-sectional versus longitudinal studies; (2) the effect of subject dropout (experimental mortality) in longitudinal studies; and (3) the issue of relating the effect of physiological pathology, such as cardiovascular disease, to normal age change in cognitive function.

Age differences versus age changes. The issues related to interpreting data obtained from cross-sectional, longitudinal or the newer sequential data-collection strategies cannot be presented here in detail (see Baltes, Reese, and Nesselroade, 1977; Friedrich and Van Horn, 1976; Schaie, 1970, 1973, 1977). Nevertheless, we would be remiss if we did not attend at least briefly to the research designs commonly used in the literature on intellectual development.

The discussion on whether and when decrement in intellectual functioning in older adults occurs is often blurred by a lack of understanding of the kind of information that is to be gleaned from different data sets. Most of the older studies have involved the cross-sectional method where, at one point in time, individuals are compared from two or more age groups who, by definition, must belong to different birth cohorts and consequently will differ somewhat in life experience. Single-cohort longitudinal studies, by contrast, compare the same individuals over two or more points in time. The former method confounds ontogenetic change with generational differences; the latter confounds ontogenetic change with the effects of sociocultural change occurring between times of measurement. These confounds are substantial for most behavioral variables, and it is unlikely that findings of cross-sectional age differences will agree with longitudinal age changes (Schaie, 1965, 1967). Consequently, many age differences reported in the literature should be interpreted as generational differences, and results from single-cohort longitudinal studies of human behavior as primarily historical accounts of the life history of a particular generation (Schaie, 1972; Schaie and Gribbin, 1975a).

To deal with the above problems, a number of alternative strategies have been suggested which have become known as *sequential* methods. These methods make it possible to estimate the effects of age, cohort and period effects more precisely. The interested reader will want to consult the references cited above for more detail. But we wish to leave the reader with the notion that results of studies which do not use the appropriate sequential method have only limited generalizability. That is, cross-sectional studies do not necessarily tell us how individuals have changed in the past, and simple longitudinal studies do not predict with certainty how people are likely to change in the future.

Experimental mortality. What we know about adult intellectual development is further limited by the problem of nonrandom dropout from panel studies upon which most of our better research findings are based. Two types of attrition seem to occur. One is related to the investigator's skill in sample maintenance as well as psychological and sociological reasons such as lack of interest, active refusal, change of residence or disappearance. The other, over which the investigator has no control, involves biological factors such as physical disease and individual differences in longevity. Studies of attrition caused by biological factors suggest that survivors excel on many positive attributes with regard to interest, attitudes, education and social status (Baltes, Schaie and Nardi, 1971; Schaie, Labouvie and Barrett, 1973).

Although one can control for attrition by comparing successive samples from the same birth cohort, each tested only once, there remain compelling reasons to continue panel studies. Only by repeatedly measuring the same individuals can one study patterns of intra-individual change, and moreover the characteristics of survivors of panel studies may well be typical for populations of special interest in settings such as adult education or professional enrichment programs.

Pathological versus normal aging. Cumulative effects of pathology are noted in aging individuals, and it is not reasonable to trace pathology-free psychological processes, except in those instances where one can demonstrate that the occurrence of a given pathology does not increase with age. When we describe intellectual development with advancing age, we would not arbitrarily exclude individuals suffering from the mild chronic conditions so common with increasing age, but we would certainly exempt from our discussion individuals suffering from acute but reversible illness. We do know that cardiovascular disease affects cognitive behavior and that such disease increases in frequency with age (Hertzog, Schaie, and Gribbin, 1978). Nevertheless, one must keep in mind that except for the very old, the majority of older adults do not suffer from significant cardiovascular disease, and that the effect of such disease upon behavior, while qualitatively and quantitatively important, does not necessarily preclude meaningful activities. A similar line of argument may, of course, be made for other less prevalent chronic diseases which increase in frequency as we age.

How Do We Measure Intelligence in Adults?

The often heard statement that intelligence is what intelligence tests measure is quite simplistic. Nevertheless, it is still important to know in what manner a person's intellectual functions are examined. In this section we will discuss what kind of norms one should use in appraising adults, the role of speed versus power tests, and differentiating performance from potential.

Age-corrected versus absolute level norms. Most intelligence tests published commercially, such as the Wechsler Adult Intelligence Scale (Matarazzo, 1972), use age-corrected norms. There are several problems with this approach if such tests are to be utilized as estimates of intellectual competence in various life situations. The most important of these is that if we are to predict behaviors of any social consequence or utility, it is not sufficient to say that an individual can perform at average level for his or her age. What must be known is whether the performance is at a level appropriate to the criterion of interest. Thus, if the criterion variable to be predicted is geared to the needs and abilities of young adults, then one should also consider the performance of the older person in terms of test norms designed for young adults. On the other hand, it does not make sense to compare young and old adults on the same norms, if given test variables have differential importance in predicting the same criterion at different life stages.

All age-corrected norms found in the literature have been developed from cross-sectional studies and are thus cohort-specific. That is, as the norms age, they will overestimate level of performance on tests where there are positive generational trends and underestimate performance on tests where there are unfavorable trends over time. It is to be hoped that test manuals developed in the future will begin to provide adult norms in terms of the birth years for which specific norms were developed, rather than the age range, in order to overcome this problem. (See Schaie and Parham, 1975, for an example of cohort-specific norms.)

Speeded versus power tests. Tests of intelligence have traditionally utilized two different format approaches. Power tests contain a series of items scaled in increasing order of difficulty, and items are presented to the examinee until a prescribed number of successive items are failed. For practical purposes, however, and particularly in group-administered tests, some time limit is generally imposed. In the latter case one speaks of a slightly speeded power test. Speeded tests present the examinee with a large number of items of approximately equal difficulty, all within the scope of performance of the examinee. The examinee's performance measured on such tests is the number of items completed within a specified period of time.

One of the well-documented facts of adult development is the slowing of response speed (Welford, 1977). This phenomenon should not have any effect upon pure power tests, and some have argued that therefore older adults should only be examined by means of power tests. Nevertheless, one aspect of competent intellectual performance is the ability to make an organized response with reasonable temporal contiguity to the stimulus which requires the response. The question in ability testing, therefore, is to ask whether or not speed of response, and how much speed, is required for adaptive behavior in a particular situation. Obviously speeded tests should be used with older individuals only if the specific question to be asked requires the assessment of the rapidity of making a motor or other response.

More complex issues arise with the slightly speeded power test. Some of the factor-analytic work with the WAIS has shown that a given subtest which was a good measure of the intended construct for young adults may become a measure of response speed for the old (Reinert, 1970). Time limits in this case must be relaxed sufficiently to permit the aged individual to tell us whether or not the problem can be solved rather than whether it is solved in a time interval which may be optimal for the young but not within the response capability of the old. Tests should be developed where speed of response is not a critical element of successful performance, and we ought to consider, as well, removing those constraints which will tend to decrease speed of response, such as inappropriately small type size, anxiety-inducing instructions, and so on.

Performance versus potential. Presently existing tools for the assessment of intellectual competence and new techniques specifically designed for the older adult, of course, do no more than provide us with estimates of current performance. But a more important question may often be whether or not older persons are likely to gain and show growth as a consequence of participation in some intervention program. Although determination of a minimally acceptable level of current performance may be essential, it may also be important to know what can be expected in terms of further intellectual development. Such determination would ordinarily require longitudinal data about individuals, but inferences from other sources may be possible. Some work has been done on the prediction of stability or change in intellectual functions from knowledge of individuals' life styles (Schaie and Gribbin, 1975b). Other promising avenues are concerned with the assessment of individuals' responses to brief experimental paradigms involving cognitive training (e.g., Labouvie-Vief and Gonda, 1976; Plemons, Willis, and Baltes, 1978).

EMPIRICAL FINDINGS

We are now ready to consider the empirical literature on age changes in intelligence. I shall proceed to do so by providing a brief summary of the work with the familiar Wechsler intelligence test and then indicate that much of the literature is methodologically deficient and thus scarcely useful for broad inference. I will then, in an admittedly parochial manner, give a much more extensive presentation of the work on the Primary Mental Abilities Test conducted by myself and my associates (See Schaie, 1979a, for a more detailed account). This section will be concluded by describing briefly how health and environmental factors interact with cognitive change.

But before we examine the research literature, there is one other issue that must be commented on, because it may well explain the hidden agenda behind some of the current discussions on the reality or myth of intellectual decrement in old age (e.g., Baltes and Schaie, 1976; Botwinick, 1977; Horn and Donaldson, 1976). This issue is concerned with the age range to be reviewed when dealing with age decrement and intelligence. The house of gerontology encompasses both scientists who are interested in the process of adult development and those interested in the end product of this development, the elderly. It is not surprising, therefore, that the first group of investigators would be interested in changes occurring past a maturational asymptote, say in the early twenties, and would pursue such changes until that stage, perhaps no later than the early seventies, where study populations can be found that are reasonably free from confounding pathology. The second group, on the other hand, would perhaps wish to start with individuals in their fifties and continue to that level where any assessable subjects at all can be found. Botwinick (1977) therefore suggests that those who focus on the earlier "developmental" ages will also argue for "no decline," while those who focus primarily on the later years will propose that "decline" is to be found.

Matters are not quite that simple, however, because the question is not just whether decline can be established for some variables for some individuals, for indeed it can. What we need to recognize instead is that there may be some variables on which there is little or no decrement and that there are some individuals who show no decrement on most variables into very old age (Baltes and Schaie, 1976; Schaie, 1974). Considering the latter statement, it becomes clear why it is most difficult to obtain data on normative aging beyond the late sixties, since most available samples will not be comparable to younger populations in terms of education, health status and other demographic variables. Separate studies with measures validated for the old are therefore needed to build appropriate normative bases (e.g., Schaie, 1978), but such studies have only begun and do not as yet allow firm conclusions. With respect to currently available data then, we must perforce take a conservative position and regard normative "decline" with a due amount of suspicion.

Wechsler Test Data on Intellectual Changes with Age

The Wechsler Adult Intelligence Test (most research on which has been done with the form known as the WAIS) is a battery of 11 factorially complex measures. Six involve primarily verbal behaviors and are called a Verbal Scale, and five involve some manipulative performance of a primarily nonverbal nature which are summed to arrive at a Performance Scale. Although the Wechsler tests first appeared in 1939, normative data for individuals beyond age 60 did not appear until 1955 (Doppelt and Wallace, 1955). Table 4.1 (adapted from Matarazzo, 1972, p. 354) presents age differences from early adulthood to late middle age. Considering that the mean of the standardization reference group is 10 and its standard deviation 3, none of the differences are particularly remarkable, but they are consistent indeed. All of the differences which approach significance involve measures which are speeded; that is, a constant time interval will with successive age groups become more and more inadequate to assess the psychological construct of interest in an equitable manner. For the power tests: Information, Comprehension, Arithmetic, Similarities and Vocabulary, there are obviously no significant changes over the entire mid-life period. Note that until 60 or so there is virtually no drop for the Verbal Scale. On the other hand, there is quite a sharp drop on the Performance Scale.

Norms for the WAIS for ages 65 and older were reported by Doppelt and Wallace (1955). These norms do show significant decline, even for verbal scales, past the age of 70. Substantial decline is most

Table 4.1. Mean Scores By Age for Subtest Performance on the WAIS During Middle Adulthood.*

	\multicolumn{5}{c}{AGE RANGE}
SUBTEST	20–24	25–34	35–44	45–54	55–64
VERBAL SCALE					
Information	9.8	10.3	10.3	9.9	9.9
Comprehension	10.0	10.2	10.2	9.9	9.6
Arithmetic	10.0	10.1	10.2	9.8	9.4
Similarities	10.2	10.1	9.2	9.0	9.0
Digit span	9.9	10.0	9.6	9.0	8.4
Vocabulary	9.6	10.3	10.4	10.1	10.1
PERFORMANCE SCALE					
Digit symbol	10.1	9.9	8.5	7.5	6.3
Picture completion	10.1	10.0	9.8	8.6	8.0
Block design	9.9	10.0	9.4	8.5	7.7
Picture arrangement	10.5	9.7	9.1	8.0	7.3
Object assembly	10.1	10.0	9.3	8.5	7.8

NOTE: Each mean is based on $n = 200$.
* Adapted from *Wechsler's Measurement and Appraisal of Adult Intelligence* by Joseph D. Matarazzo, 5th and enlarged edition. Copyright © 1939, 1941, 1944, 1958 by David Wechsler; 1972 by Oxford University Press, Inc. Reprinted by permission of author and Oxford University Press, Inc.

noteworthy again for the performance (speed-implicated) measures. This discrepancy incidentally seems well replicated and has been found across the sexes, racial groups, and different socioeconomic levels (Eisdorfer, Busse and Cohen, 1959). Greater than average decline in performance IQ has been implicated as a predictor of survival (Hall et al., 1972). In another study, Harwood and Naylor (1971) matched a group of subjects in their sixties and seventies with a young adult control group in terms of the overall WAIS IQ. For the group of persons in their sixties, Information, Comprehension and Vocabulary scores were higher than for the matched young, in which Digit, Symbol, Picture Completion, and Picture Arrangement were lower. The same pattern held for the group in their seventies except that now Object Assembly as well was lower than for the young adult controls. But for some elderly, relaxation of time limits may change this pattern (Storandt, 1977).

While cross-sectional comparisons of the WAIS clearly implicate speed-related age decrements beyond the fifties, it has generally been maintained that verbal performance continues unimpaired into old age. This notion was challenged by Botwinick and Storandt (1974) who gave the WAIS Vocabulary Test to individuals ranging in age from 62 to 83 years who were matched on quantitative scores for that test. Qualitative scoring then revealed that the younger subjects excelled in superior synonyms (the only scoring category yielding an age difference). But in a similar later study (Botwinick, West, and Storandt, 1975) the authors concluded that qualitative and quantitative age differences in Vocabulary performance did not differ except for fine nuances of meanings.

Eisdorfer and Wilkie (1973) have reported longitudinal data on changes in WAIS scores over a 10-year period for groups of subjects in their sixties and seventies, each tested four times. A small number of subjects had three further tests over an additional 5-year period. The 10-year loss between the sixties and seventies was statistically significant but amounted only to an average of 2 score points for the Performance and 0.6 for the Verbal Scales. From the seventies to the eighties there was a total loss of 7.3 score points about equally divided between Verbal and Performance Scales. Similar declines from the mid-sixties into the eighties were reported in a 20-year study by Blum, Fossnage and Jarvik (1972). By contrast, there have been some reports on highly selected groups which show little or no drop on Vocabulary even into very advanced age (Gilbert, 1973; Green, 1969). Further comprehensive studies involving short-term longitudinal follow-up conducted with psychiatric and community samples are reported in a monograph by Savage, Britton, Bolton, and Hall (1973). Their findings generally echo those reviewed above but, in addition, call attention to both quantitative and qualitative differences in age changes in normal community-dwelling individuals and those with identified psychopathology. Performance Scale deficit is seen as a specific predictor of lessened longevity, while changes in the Verbal Scale have primarily individual nonnormative significance.

Age Changes on the Primary Mental Abilities Test

The Wechsler subtests are factorially complex. A clearer picture may therefore be obtained by considering age differences for the factorially less complex Primary Mental Abilities Test (Thurstone and Thurstone, 1949). Results of the first parametric study of this test covering the age range from early adulthood to early old age (Schaie, 1958) are shown in Figure 4.1. These data come from a study of 25 men and 25 women in each 5-year interval from ages 20 to 70 who were randomly selected from the membership of a large metropolitan prepaid health-care plan. This sample also provides the base for the sequential studies to be discussed in this section. Five abilities were systematically sampled: Verbal Meaning (V), a measure of recognition vocabulary; Space (S), the ability to visualize mentally the rotation of geometric objects; Reasoning (R), a measure of the ability to identify rules and serial principles; Number (N), a test of numerical skills; and Word Fluency (W), a measure of vocabulary recall.

Inspection of Figure 4.1 reveals only insubstantial age differences until about age 50 for Space, Reasoning and Verbal Meaning, and until about age 60 for Number and for Word Fluency. For the latter, even at age 70 the drop from peak does not exceed 1 standard deviation. Note also that adult peaks obtain for most abilities for the 31–35-year-old group.

The basic flaw of cross-sectional studies, as was pointed out earlier in this chapter, is the fact that such studies confound age changes with

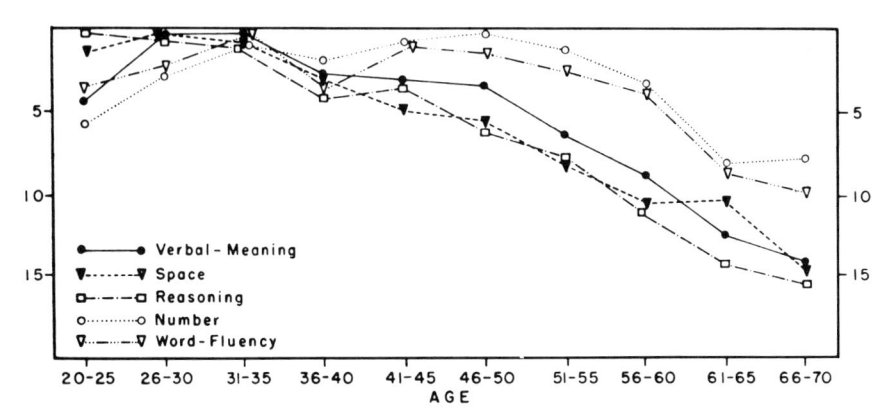

Figure 4.1. Mean decrement in the primary mental abilities from mean peak levels in T-score points. (From: Schaie, K. W. Rigidity-flexibility and intelligence: A cross-sectional study of the adult life-span from 20 to 70. *Psychological Monographs,* **72:** No. 462 (Whole No. 9), 1958. Copyright 1958 by the American Psychological Association. Reprinted by permission.)

generational differences. It becomes important therefore to examine age trends determined by following samples of individuals over time supplemented by longitudinal studies based on independent samples, that is successive samples drawn from the same birth cohort at different ages but tested only once.

We were fortunate to be able to retest members of our 1956 samples after 7, 14 and 21 years and to obtain new panels in 1963 and 1970 from the same population frame. The 1963 panel was retested in 1970 and 1977, and the 1970 panel was retested in 1977. Only initial analyses, however, are as yet complete for our 1977 data wave.

The following sections will summarize findings for the five primary abilities as well as for composite measures suggested by the Thurstones (1949, 1958). These are a composite measure of Intellectual Ability (IA = V + S + 2R + 2N + W) and an Index of Educational Aptitude (EA = 2V + R).

Data from Panel Studies

The first longitudinal follow-up. In this study 303 persons from the 1956 panel were reexamined in 1963. While there was substantial replication of cross-sectional findings, means at comparable ages were systematically higher in 1963 than in 1956 for all variables except for Word Fluency, where the opposite pattern prevailed. And, when we examined the longitudinal age changes it became clear that, again with the exception of Word Fluency, ontogenetic changes were minimal until the sixties. Even then they appear to be largest, in contrast to the cross-sectional findings, for Word Fluency, and are quite small for Reasoning, Space, Number and Verbal Meaning.

Our next concern was with the problems of constructing appropriate gradients which permit comparison between cross-sectional and longitudinal findings. We argued that the best comparison would occur by contrasting short-term longitudinal data with cross-sectional data averaged over the time interval bounding the longitudinal segments. For purposes of age-gradient construction we combined data from both sexes, and to reduce sampling variability, we calculated age changes for successive 5-year age intervals averaged over each pair of successive cohorts. Figure 4.2 provides graphic representations of the estimated average cross-sectional and composite longitudinal gradients. These graphs compare age gradients obtained on the basis of current performance of individuals at different ages who are members of *different* cohorts with the estimated longitudinal age gradient for a *single* cohort. If age differences were attributable solely to maturational or otherwise age-related causes, then gradients constructed in either manner ought to coincide. But if cross-sectional differences include differences in experience or talent between successive cohorts, then the two gradients must diverge. If generational differences go in a positive direction, then the cross-sectional, between generation difference, gradient must be below the longitudinal, within generation, gradient. Conversely, unfavorable change across generations will yield cross-sectional gradients above the longitudinal gradient.

Figure 4.2 reveals positive intergenerational differences for Verbal Meaning, Space and Reasoning, and to a lesser degree for Number. Negative generational differences are shown for Word Fluency. As is generally true for omnibus measures of intellectual ability, ours included, no differences were found between cross-sectional and longitudinal gradients on the composite Intellectual Ability measure because the effects of positive and negative generational differences have been averaged. The Index of Education Aptitude, however, showed positive intergenerational differences, being a composite of measures for which similar findings occur.

The second longitudinal follow-up. Of the panel members retested in 1963, it was possible to reexamine 162 in 1970. In addition, we were also able to get 7-year data on 418 of the individuals who had first entered the study in 1963. Two separate issues could not be addressed on the basis of short-term longitudinal data. Once again we were in a position to describe within-subject age changes for a series of seven successive 7-year cohorts, but now over a 14-year time period (Schaie and Labouvie-Vief, 1974). Of equal interest, however, is the replication of 7-year changes within subjects for two independent samples carried during two successive time periods. It is this latter comparison which permits application of the cohort-sequential method and, thus, a direct test of the relative contribution of age and cohort variance (Schaie and Parham, 1977).

The 14-year data can be conceptualized as the simultaneous longitudinal study from 1956 to 1970 of seven cohorts, successively differ-

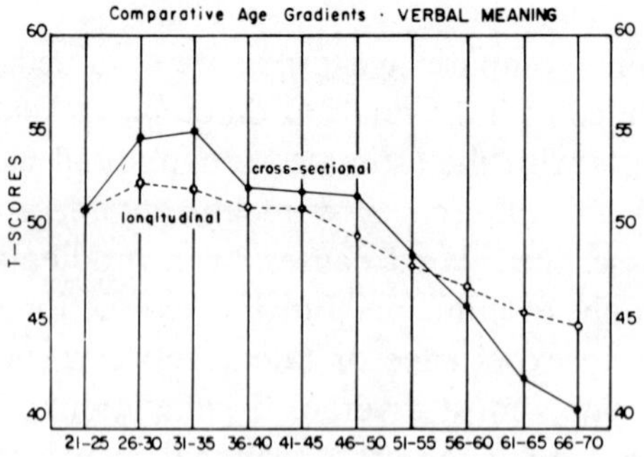
Comparative Age Gradients · VERBAL MEANING
T-SCORES
cross-sectional
longitudinal
AGE

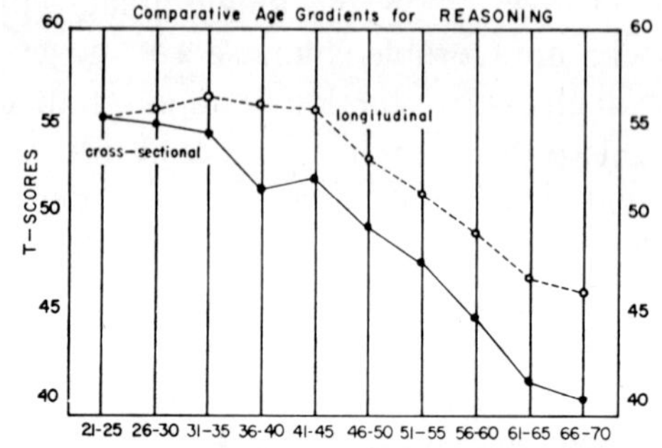
Comparative Age Gradients for REASONING
T-SCORES
longitudinal
cross-sectional

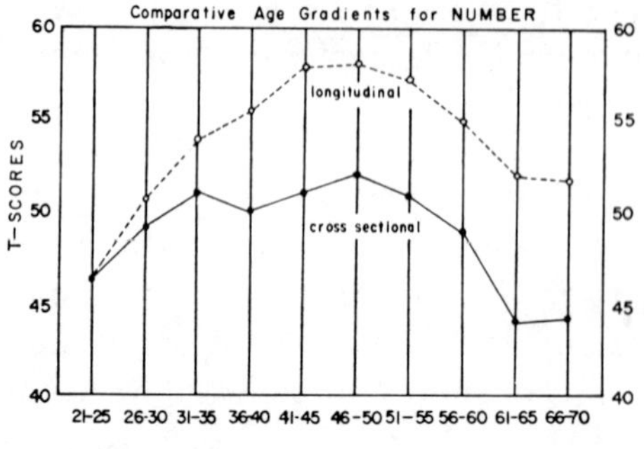
Comparative Age Gradients for NUMBER
T-SCORES
longitudinal
cross sectional

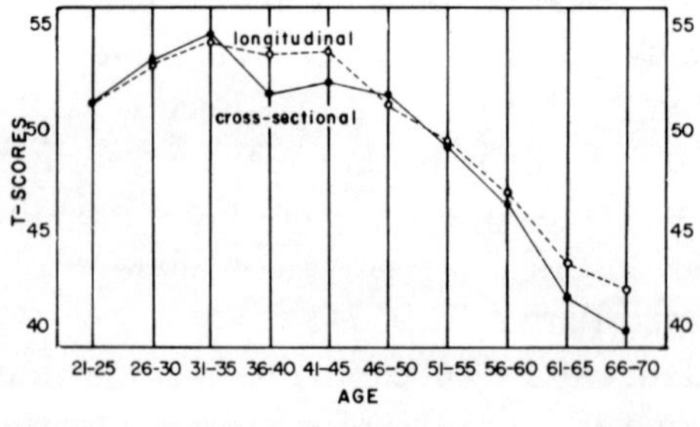
Comparative Age Gradients · INTELLECTUAL ABILITY
T-SCORES
longitudinal
cross-sectional
AGE

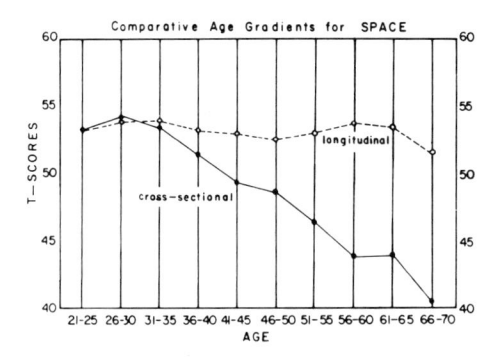

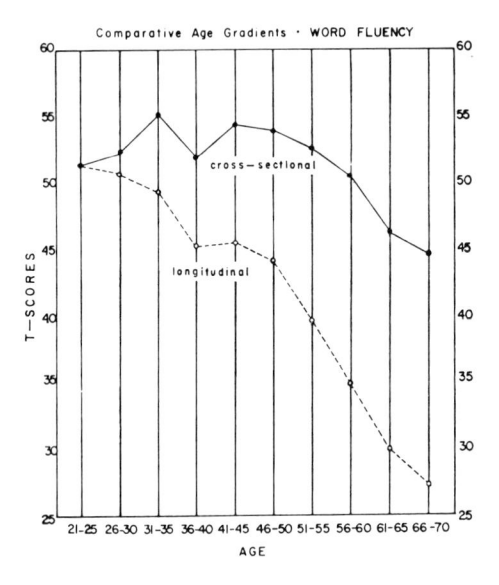

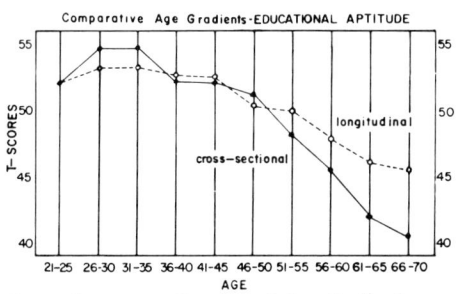

Figure 4.2. Comparison of cross-sectional and longitudinal age gradients. (From: Schaie and Strother, 1968b. Copyright by Multivariate Behavioral Research. Reprinted by permission.)

ing by 7 years in average birthdate. The oldest cohort, with average birth year 1889, is followed from mean age 67 to mean age 81; the youngest cohort, with average birth year 1938, is followed from mean age 25 to mean age 39; and so on. Results of this analysis plotted along a chronological age scale are provided by Figure 4.3.

The substantial effects of cohort differences become apparent immediately. But attention is focused also on the many differences in ontogenetic pattern by type of ability as well as cohort membership. Reliable decrement ($p < 0.01$) over a 14-year period is observed for Space and Reasoning only for the oldest cohort from mean age 67 to mean age 81. No reliable 14-year change is found for Number. For Verbal Meaning, however, reliable decrement is observed for both oldest and second oldest cohorts, that is, as early as from age 60 to 74. For Word Fluency, decrement is found for all but the two youngest cohorts, that is, beginning from age 39 to 53. Reliable decrement on the composite IQ measure is seen for the three oldest cohorts, from age 53, but for the measure of Educational Aptitude, only for the two oldest cohorts, from age 60. In addition, reliable 14-year increment from 25 to 39 is found for the youngest cohort for Verbal Meaning and Educational Aptitude.

The 7-year data in this study represent a direct replication of the first follow-up study. Even clearer patterns appeared here for the age/cohort relationship shown in our first study for Verbal Meaning, Space, Reasoning and the composite indexes. For Number there is partial replication, this time without the finding of apparent negative cohort effects for the youngest cohort. However, there is apparent failure to replicate our earlier finding of substantial ontogenetic changes on Word Fluency in early middle age. It is apparent then that the longitudinal findings for the first follow-up may have reflected (for the younger cohorts) negative time-of-measurement rather than age-decrement effects.

These data clearly support our contention of the late onset and relatively limited evidence for ontogenetic decrement in healthy populations. Arguments to the contrary advanced by Horn and Donaldson (1976) involve the application of inappropriate statistical procedures and cannot be taken seriously (see also Baltes and Schaie, 1976; Schaie and Baltes, 1977). Horn and Donaldson do, however, correctly point to discrepancies in findings between the panel studies and the estimates derived from independent samples. That question will be addressed next.

Independent Samples Data

Experimental mortality. The above findings must be tempered by the effects of selective attrition which limit the degree to which findings from panel studies can be generalized. Our data base permits assessing the effect of attrition by contrasting base scores for participants and dropouts from the same cohorts who had entered the study in either 1956 or 1963 (Schaie, Labouvie, and Barrett, 1973).

Significant participation effects were found for all variables. As shown by Figure 4.4., participants consistently get higher mean scores, with the exception of the two youngest cohorts, on Number, Word Fluency and the composite Intellectual Ability measures. The differences between retest participants and dropouts, however, is more pronounced for the older cohorts. In fact, significant age-by-cohort interactions were found for Verbal Meaning, Number and the composite indexes. In addition, there was less pronounced participation by time-of-measurement effects for Verbal Meaning and the Index of Educational Aptitude in the direction of greater differences between retest participants and dropouts in 1963. What is apparent then is that the discrepancies between numbers of the longitudinal panel and random samples from the parent population tend to increase over time.

One way in which the issue of panel attrition can be addressed is to obtain independent samples at each measurement point from each cohort of interest. This requires, of course, additional draws of new cross-sectional panels as was done in our studies. Interestingly enough, such data seem to differ from panel data primarily in level of function and for some variables in the age range of onset of reliable decrement (Schaie and Strother, 1968b; Schaie, Labouvie, and Buech, 1973). It is our impression at this time that the panel data are representative of stable populations of healthy upper- and middle-class individuals, while the independent samples data may be more representative of unselected samples from the general populations. Differences between the two types of data bases may be more important when one addresses the issue of magnitude of age changes in intelligence.

64

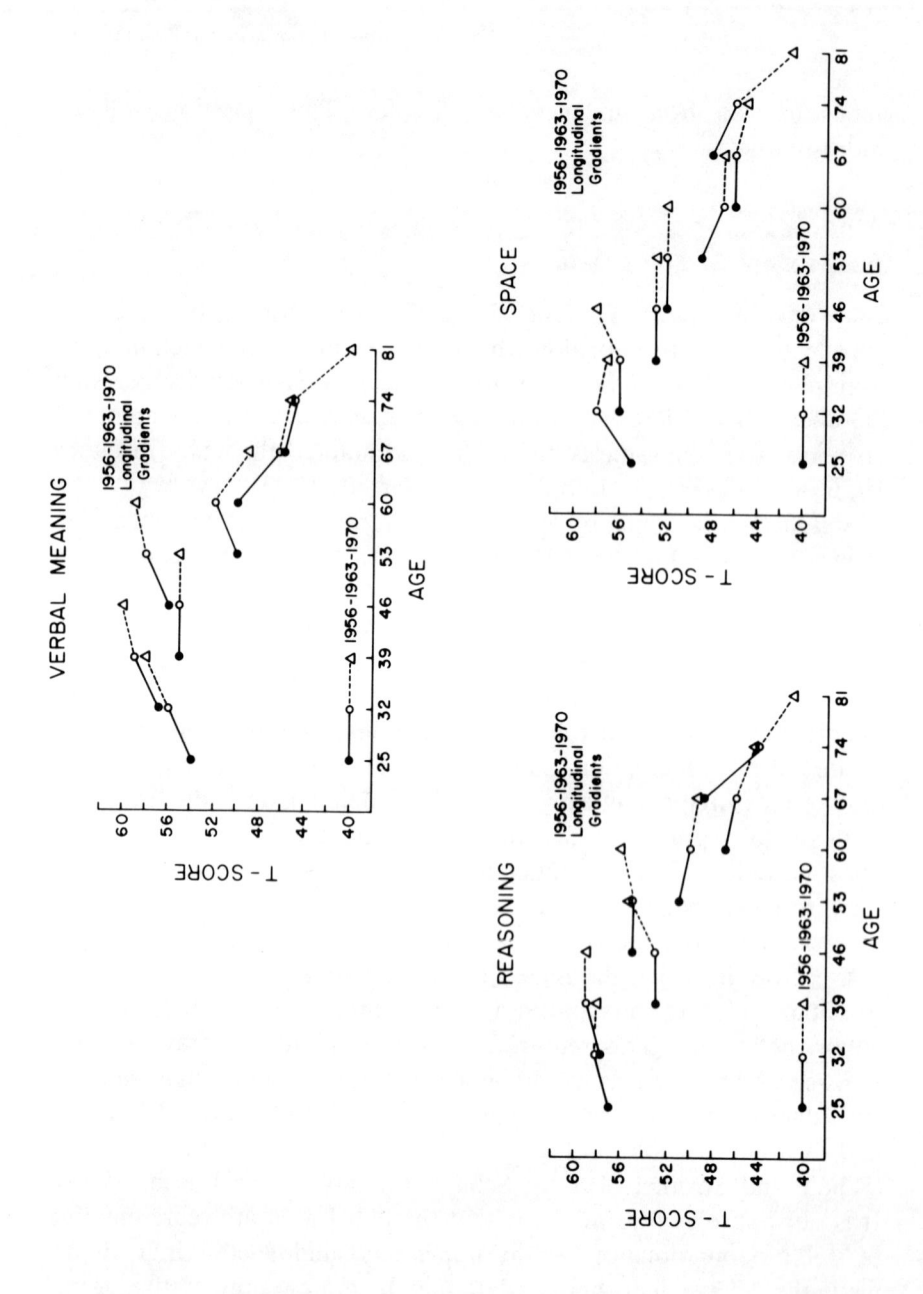

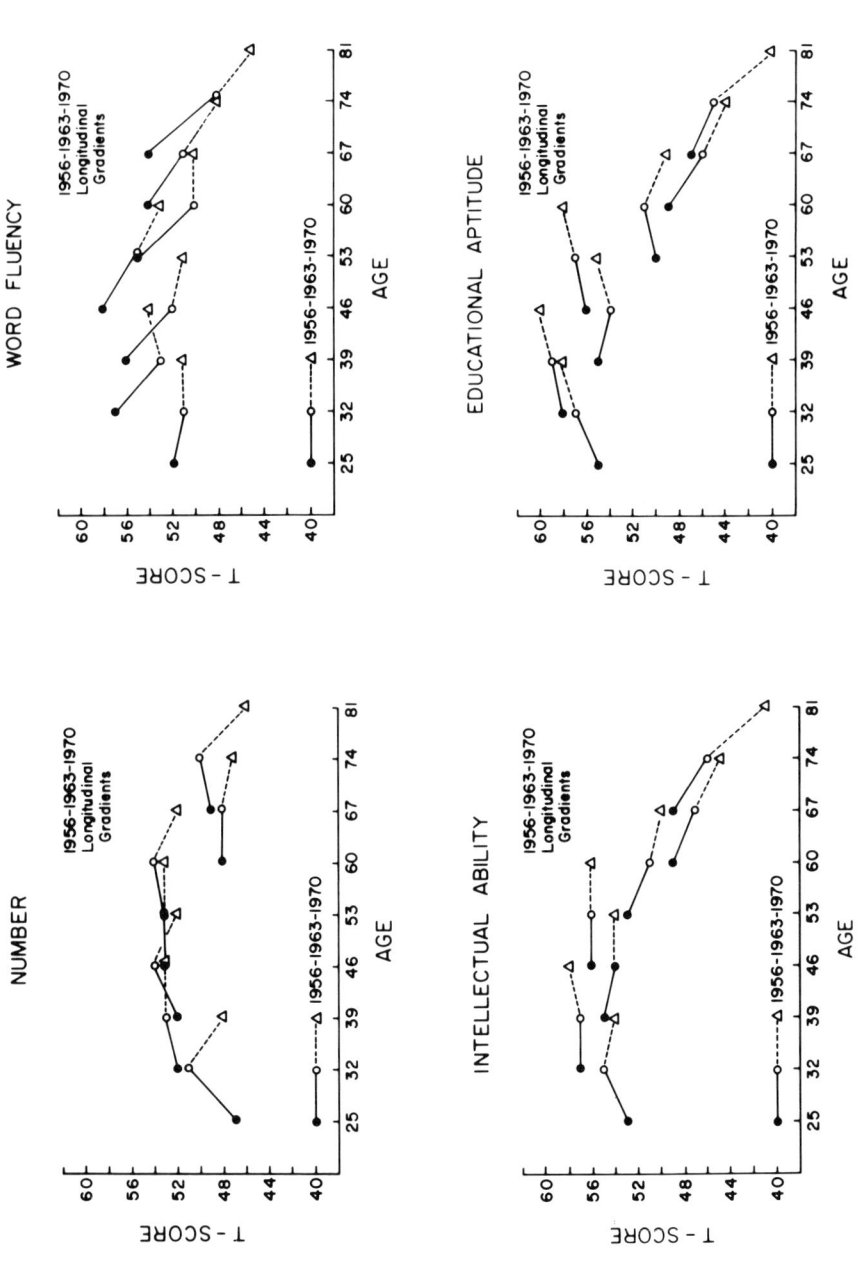

Figure 4.3. Mean scores by cohort for the 14-year longitudinal study. (From: Schaie, K. W., and Labouvie-Vief, G. Generational versus ontogenetic components of change in adult cognitive behavior: A fourteen-year cross-sequential study. Developmental Psychology, **10**: 305–320, 1974. Copyright 1974 by the American Psychological Association. Reprinted by permission.)

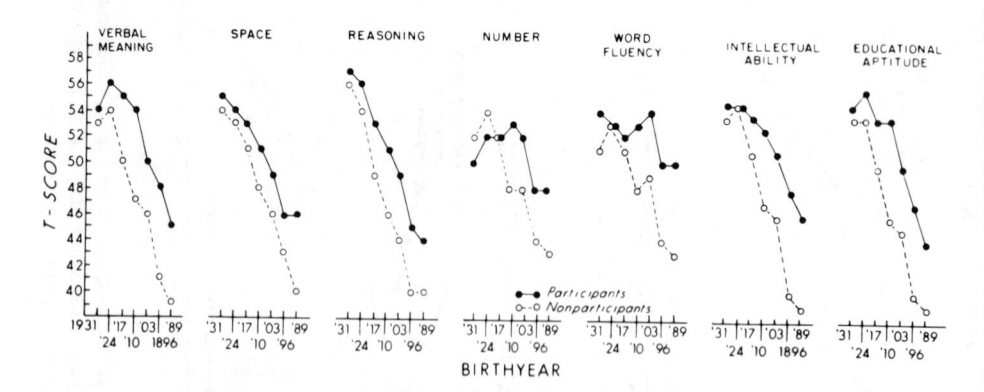

Figure 4.4. Cohort differences for retest participants and dropouts. (From: Schaie, Labouvie, and Barrett, 1973. Copyright by *Journal of Gerontology*. Reprinted by permission.)

Magnitude of age changes. As scientists, we are concerned about demonstrating the presence or absence of reliable differences or relationships. What is frequently ignored, however, is the question of whether or not such differences are substantial enough to warrant our advice to those who wish to implement public policy or other practical matters on the basis of our findings. In this section we will examine specific estimates of age changes within cohorts over 7-year intervals from 25 to 81 years and similar estimates of cohort differences for cohorts with average birth years from 1889 to 1938 (see also Schaie and Parham, 1977).

The issue of practical consequence was addressed more directly by summing cumulative age changes as proportions of performance level for the samples tested at age 25. This was done by adding successive within-cohort changes averaged across the two 7-year intervals for which data were available. In the case of the repeated measurement data, this would tend to yield rather conservative estimates favoring decrement finding because of the expected tendency of a panel consisting of favorably selected members (because of nonrandom attrition) to regress toward the sample mean (see Baltes, Nesselroade, and Labouvie, 1972).

A convenient and reasonable approach to appraising the practical significance of cumulative age changes and/or cohort differences is to take recourse in the traditional assumption that 1 Probable Error

(PE) about the mean defines the middle 59% (average) range of performance on mental abilities, assuming normal distribution within the population (Matarazzo, 1972, pp. 124–126). Using this criterion, cumulative decrement in performance could be judged to be of practical importance in that instance where such cumulative loss reduces the performance of the older sample to a level more than 1 PE below the mean (i.e., drop to the lower quartile) of the young adult base.

Table 4.2 charts performance in 7-year intervals for ages 32 to 81 as a proportion of performance at age 25. Note that in the first study, based on panel members who remain after some of the less favorably endowed individuals have dropped out, within-cohort level of performance was found to be below the mid-range of 25-year-olds at age 67 for Word Fluency and at age 81 for Inductive Reasoning and the Index of Intellectual Aptitude, with no drop below this point for the remaining variables. By contrast, when projecting from the inde-

Table 4.2. Index of Age Change Rounded to Integers.*

VARIABLE		32	39	46	53	60	67	74	81	−1 PE AT AGE 25
Verbal meaning	R	107	112	116	119	120	117	110	103	84
	I	102	102	100	95	95	89	80	74	83
Spatial	R	113	114	117	118	117	110	97	77	71
visualization	I	98	90	89	82	81	68	58	55	71
Inductive	R	94	97	97	95	96	91	82	74	80
reasoning	I	97	90	84	76	72	64	58	53	79
Number	R	110	114	115	116	120	116	103	89	71
	I	116	119	121	115	115	106	98	85	74
Word fluency	R	100	96	95	89	86	74	63	52	83
	I	96	89	85	77	74	60	50	46	82
Intellectual	R	107	106	110	109	109	103	93	81	84
ability	I	103	99	97	90	88	79	70	63	84
Educational	R	107	112	116	117	118	115	108	101	85
aptitude	I	101	100	97	92	91	84	76	70	83

NOTE: Base: age 25 = 100; R = repeated measurement panel; I = independent sample.
* From: Schaie, K. W., and Parham, I. A. Cohort-sequential analysis of adult intellectual development (extended version of Schaie and Parham, 1977), NAPS No. 03170.

pendent samples, which are, of course, more representative of the population at large, performance has already dropped below the 25-year average range at age 53 for Inductive Reasoning and Word Fluency, at age 67 for Space and the Index of Intellectual Ability, and at age 74 for Verbal Meaning and the Index of Educational Aptitude.

Health and Environmental Factors

Thus far, we have demonstrated that age decrement is not as great or uniform as popular stereotypes would have us believe and that generational (cohort) differences must be taken seriously. But what is the nature of these cohort differences? One can identify a variety of intrinsic and extrinsic variables by which generations, however defined, do differ. Thus far, we have seriously looked at some gross demographic indicators, have conducted an analysis of cumulative health trauma and have engaged in the study of interpersonal environments.

Demographic factors. These issues were first addressed after the initial cross-sectional study when we became aware of the fact that there were significant cohort differences on such obvious demographic variables as income, education and occupational status. Analysis of covariance was used to partial out the effects of these demographic variables on the mental ability scores (Schaie, 1959). As could be expected, age-difference effects were reduced but not eliminated. The fact we are dealing with, of course, is that the demographic variables are differentially distributed across cohorts; that is, the level of education or income in one cohort does not have the identical meaning of that found in another.

Health history factors. More recently, we have investigated the effect of cumulative health trauma on change in intellectual functions. Clinic or hospital contacts of 150 of our participants were charted by the appropriate code from the International Classification of Diseases (ICDA) (U.S. Public Health Service, 1968). Although the ICDA contains over 8000 classifications, only about 820 were actually encountered. Collapsing overlapping categories permitted further reduction to 448 classifications, which were then Q-sorted by 12 physicians (six internal medicine and six psychiatry residents) on an 11-point scale ranging from benign to extremely severe, in terms of the impact of each disease entity upon the future health and well-being of the patient (Parham, Gribbin, Hertzog, and Schaie, 1975). To our initial surprise, we found only minor relations between cumulative health trauma and mental abilities. These low-level effects occurred for Verbal Meaning and Word Fluency, but only when severity-weighted disease episodes were considered. It is of interest to note that at least some variance in verbal behavior decrement can be accounted for on the basis of physical disease.

Further investigations were pursued on individuals with known cardiovascular disease. Several interesting findings occurred as we engaged in the detailed analysis of 155 panel members who had been followed over a 14-year period. At first glance cardiovascular disease results in lowered function on all variables monitored. However, when we control for cohort (age), the effect is no longer significant for either Space or Word Fluency; and when socioeconomic status is taken into consideration, the effect is found only for Number and the composite Index of Intellectual Ability. What this means is that cardiovascular disease is more prevalent in members of older cohorts and those of lower socioeconomic status, who also perform lower on the Primary Mental Abilities Test. While cardiovascular disease, therefore, does indeed contribute to cognitive decline, the variance accounted for is not large, and there are likely to be indirect rather than specific causal effects. For example, cardiovascular disease may lead to changes in life-style which more directly affect cognitive function (Hertzog, Schaie, and Gribbin, 1978). It is conceivable also that less healthy life-styles shown by individuals of low education and intellectual ability might have modest causal effect upon the development of cardiovascular disease.

Environmental factors. The effect of environmental factors upon both level of performance and change across age on the mental abilities was studied further by examining our participants' microenvironment. A Life-Complexity Inventory (LCI) was used to interview 140 individuals who had been followed for 14 years. Initial analysis of the LCI yielded eight item clusters representing: 1) subjective dissatisfaction with life status, 2) level of social status, 3) a noisy environment, 4) family dissolution, 5) disengagement from interaction with the environment, 6) semi- or passive-engagement with the environment, 7) maintenance of acculturation, and 8) female homemaker activities.

Correlations were computed between LCI cluster scores and the level of intellectual performance at each of our three data points. Positive correlations were found between all ability variables and the social status cluster, and similarly negative correlations occurred throughout the disengagement cluster. In addition, Verbal Meaning, Word Fluency and Educational Aptitude related positively to maintenance of acculturation; family dissolution correlated negatively with Reasoning and Educational Aptitude; female homemaker role correlated negatively with Space; dissatisfaction with life status related negatively to the Intellectual Ability Index and Number; and noisy environment correlated positively with Word Fluency (Gribbin, Schaie, and Parham, 1975). An additional analysis showed that high disengagement and family-dissolution cluster scores were associated with cognitive decrement over a 14-year period (Schaie and Gribbin, 1975b).

CONCLUDING COMMENTS

In the final section of this chapter I would like to summarize my evaluation of the present status of the question of intellectual decline with age and alert the reader to the fact that we have thus far studied intellectual changes in old age with instruments designed for the young.

The Current Status of the Question of Intellectual Decline with Age

When all the evidence presented in this chapter is weighed and due consideration is given to recent reanalyses of some of these data by others (Botwinick, 1977; Horn and Donaldson, 1976), it is hoped that the reader will come to agree with certain conclusions I will now attempt to summarize. First, it is clear that reliable decrement until very old age (and by that I mean late eighties) cannot be found for all abilities or for all individuals. Second, it is equally clear that for most individuals there is decrement on those abilities which require speed of response, and for those abilities whose measurement is particularly sensitive to relatively modest impairment of the peripheral nervous system. Third, decrement is also likely to be found on most abilities for individuals with severe cardiovascular disease at any age, and for individuals living in relatively undifferentiated or socially deprived environments beginning with the late fifties and early sixties.

Fourth, data from independent random samples (including cross-sectional studies) will tend to overestimate "normal" age decrements for those variables where ontogenetic changes indeed occur, because sampling procedures will tend to include individuals performing at lower levels not because of age, but because of ability-related disease and/or life-style variables. Data from longitudinal and repeated-measurement sequential studies will accurately estimate age changes for individuals living under relatively favorable environmental conditions and in above-average health, but will overestimate performance maintenance for those living under less favorable conditions and in less than average health.

Fifth, I maintain the position that variance for ontogenetic change for most abilities is small relative to that demonstrated for cohort differences. It should be emphasized, however, that while cohort differences account for most cross-sectional age-difference variance into the mid-sixties, from then on there is a mix of cohort and age effects, with age effects assuming increasing importance as the eighties are reached.

Finally, I would like to state once again that in healthy, well-educated populations ontogenetic change on intellectual-ability variables is proportionally small, such that many individuals perform with the middle range of young adults. Generational differences in such samples also are not as pronounced as in the general population, but they do persist. And due note should be taken of the tremendous range of individual differences. Some adults show decrement on some abilities quite early in life, but others maintain their function into old age.

On Studying Intelligence in the Old with Tests Developed for the Young

A major issue we have not thus far addressed (Schaie, 1978) is the question of ecological validity. Studies of omnibus measures of intellectual competence in common use appear to be most relevant for situations which rarely, if ever, are faced by the middle-aged or the elderly. Although studies of functional unities of intelligence, such as our own work with the Primary Mental Abilities Test (Schaie, 1979a), may indeed explain most individual-difference variance in early adulthood, other abilities, those relatively unimportant in youth, require more detailed assessment in later adulthood.

What then is to be done? First, we must learn more about situations in which adults are required to display competence, and this requires a taxonomy of adult situations (Scheidt and Schaie, 1978). Next, we must construct new measures of intelligence, based upon what we now know of the structure of intellect, but which do not require that novelty be the impetus for the subject's adaptive response. Instead, the tasks to be used must be meaningful and embedded in the life experience of the adult, and moreover attuned to the need for cohort as well as age relevance (Schaie, 1978). Third, we must examine the mediating role of motivational variables and especially the effect of caution and risk taking in response to cognitive tasks (Birkhill and Schaie, 1975). And finally, we must investigate the potential generalizability of our new tasks across classes of situations and types of individuals, if we are to attain a technology which is to be scientifically valid and suitable for application to real life problems. All that has been said in this chapter, therefore, is at best a prologue and a statement reflecting the state of the art. Work in progress at some of the major gerontological centers may well change our conclusions, and much exciting work lies ahead.

REFERENCES

Baltes, P. B., Nesselroade, J. R., Schaie, K. W., and Labouvie, E. W. On the dilemma of regression effects in examining ability: Level-related differentials in ontogenetic patterns of adult intelligence. *Develop. Psychol.* **6**:78–84 (1972).

Baltes, P. B., Reese, H. W., and Nesselroade, J. R. *Life-span Developmental Psychology: An Introduction to Research Methods.* Monterey, Calif.: Brooks/Cole Publishing Co., 1977.

Baltes, P. B., and Schaie, K. W. The myth of the twilight years. *Psychol. Today:* 35–40 (March 1974).

Baltes, P. B., and Schaie, K. W. On the plasticity of intelligence in adulthood and old age: where Horn and Donaldson fail. *Amer. Psychol.* **31**:725-730 (1976).

Baltes, P. B., Schaie, K. W., and Nardi, A. H. Age and experimental mortality in a seven-year longitudinal study of cognitive behavior. *Develop. Psychol.* **5**:18-26 (1971).

Binet, A., and Simon, T. Le development de l'intelligence chez les enfants. *Annee Psychol.* **14**:1-94 (1908).

Birkhill, W. R., and Schaie, K. W. The effect of differential reinforcement of cautiousness in the intellectual performance of the elderly. *J. Gerontol.* **30**:578-583 (1975).

Blum, J. E., Fosshage, J. L., and Jarvik, L. F. Intellectual changes and sex differences in octogenarians: a twenty-year longitudinal study of aging. *Develop. Psychol.* **7**:178-187 (1972).

Botwinick, J. Intellectual abilities. In J. E. Birren and K. W. Schaie (eds.), *Handbook of the Psychology of Aging*. New York: Van Nostrand Reinhold Co., 1977.

Botwinick, J., and Storandt, M. Vocabulary ability in later life. *J. Genet. Psychol.* **125**:303-308 (1974).

Botwinick, J., West, R., and Storandt, M. Qualitative vocabulary test response and age. *J. Gerontol.* **30**:574-577 (1975).

Cattell, J. McK. Mental tests and their measurement. *Mind* **15**:373-380 (1890).

Cattell, R. B. Theory of fluid and crystallized intelligence: a critical experiment. *J. Educ. Psychol.* **54**:1-22 (1963).

Connolly, K. J., and Bruner, J. C. *The Growth of Competence*. New York: Academic Press, Inc., 1974.

Doppelt, J. E., and Wallace, W. L. Standardization of the Wechsler Adult Intelligence Scale for older persons. *J. Abnorm. Soc. Psychol.* **51**:312-330 (1955).

Eisdorfer, C., Busse, E. W., and Cohen, L. D. The WAIS performance of an age sample: the relationship between verbal and performance IQ's. *J. Gerontol.* **14**:197-201 (1959).

Eisdorfer, C., and Wilkie, F. Intellectual changes with advancing age. In L. F. Jarvik, C. Eisdorfer, and J. E. Blum (eds.), *Intellectual Functioning in Adults*. New York: Springer Publishing Co., Inc., 1973, pp. 21-29.

Erikson, E. H. *Insight and Responsibility*. New York: W. W. Norton & Co., Inc., 1964.

Flavell, J. H. *The Developmental Psychology of Jean Piaget*. New York: D. Van Nostrand Co., 1963.

Flavell, J. H. Cognitive changes in adulthood. In L. R. Goulet and P. B. Baltes (eds.), *Life-span Developmental Psychology: Research and Theory*. New York: Academic Press, Inc., 1970, pp. 248-257.

Friedrich, D. K., and Van Horn, K. R. *Developmental Methodology: A Revised Primer*. Minneapolis, Minn.: Burgess Publishing Co., 1976.

Galton, F. *Inquiries into Human Faculty and its Development.* London: The Macmillan Co., 1883.

Gilbert, J. G. Thirty-five year follow-up study of intellectual functioning. *J. Gerontol.* **28**:68–72 (1973).

Green, R. F. Age-intelligence relationship between ages sixteen and sixty-four: a rising trend. *Devlop. Psychol.* **1**:618–627 (1969).

Gribbin, K., Schaie, K. W., and Parham, I. A. Cognitive complexity and maintenance of intellectual abilities. Paper presented at the 10th Internat. Cong. Gerontol., Jerusalem, Israel, 1975.

Guilford, J. P. *The Nature of Human Intelligence.* New York: McGraw-Hill Book Co., 1967.

Hall, E. H., Savage, R. D., Bolton, N., Pidwell, D. M., and Blessed, G. Intellect, mental illness and survival in the aged: a longitudinal investigation. *J. Gerontol.* **27**:237–244 (1972).

Hall, G. S. *Senescence, the Last Half of Life.* New York: Appleton, 1922.

Harwood, E., and Naylor, G. F. K. Changes in the constitution of the WAIS intelligence pattern with advancing age. *Austral. J. Psychol.* **23**:297–303 (1971).

Havighurst, R. J. *Developmental Tasks and Education.* New York: David McKay Co., Inc., 1972.

Havighurst, R. Development of humanitarian concern: individualized education. In A. W. Chickering (ed.), *The Future American College.* San Francisco: Jossey-Bass, Inc., Publishers, 1979, in press.

Hertzog, C., Schaie, K. W., and Gribbin, K. Cardiovascular disease and changes in intellectual functioning from middle to old age. *J. Gerontol.* **33**:872–883 (1978).

Hollingworth, H. L. *Mental Growth and Decline: A Survey of Developmental Psychology.* New York: D. Appleton & Co., 1927.

Horn, J. L. Organization of data on life-span development in human abilities. In L. R. Goulet and P. B. Baltes (eds.), *Life-span Developmental Psychology: Research and Theory.* New York: Academic Press, Inc., 1970, pp. 424–467.

Horn, J. L., and Donaldson, G. On the myth of intellectual decline in adulthood. *Amer. Psychol.* **31**:701–719 (1976).

Horn, J. L., and Donaldson, G. Faith is not enough: a response to the Baltes-Schaie claim that intelligence does not wane. *Amer. Psychol.* **32**:369–373 (1977).

Jones, H. E., and Conrad, H. S. The growth and decline of intelligence: a study of a homogeneous group between the ages of ten and sixty. *Genet. Psychol. Monogr.* **13**:223–298 (1933).

Kohlberg, L. Continuities in childhood and adult moral development revisited. In P. B. Baltes and K. W. Schaie (eds.), *Life-span Developmental Psychology: Personality and Socialization.* New York: Academic Press, Inc., 1973, pp. 179–204.

Labouvie-Vief, G., and Gonda, J. N. Cognitive strategy training and intellectual performance in the elderly. *J. Gerontol.* **31**:327–332 (1976).
Matarazzo, J. D. *Wechsler's Measurement and Appraisal of Adult Intelligence.* Baltimore: The Williams and Wilkins Co., 1972.
Parham, I. A., Gribbin, K., Hertzog, C., and Schaie, K. W. Health status assessment by age and implications for cognitive change. Paper presented at the 10th Internat. Cong. Gerontol., Jerusalem, Israel, 1975.
Piaget, J. Intellectual evolution from adolescence to adulthood. *Human Develop.* **15**:1–12 (1972).
Plemons, J. K., Willis, S. L., and Baltes, P. B. Modifiability of fluid intelligence in aging: a short-term longitudinal training approach. *J. Gerontol.* **33**:224–231 (1978).
Pressey, S. L., Janney, J. E., and Kuhlen, R. G. *Life: A Psychological Survey.* New York: Hayer, 1939.
Reinert, G. Comparative factor analytic studies of intelligence throughout the human life-span. In L. R. Goulet and P. B. Baltes (eds.), *Life-span Developmental Psychology: Research and Theory:* New York: Academic Press, Inc., 1970.
Savage, R. D., Britton, P. G., Bolton, N., and Hall, E. H. *Intellectual Functioning in the Aged.* New York: Harper and Row, Publishers, Inc., 1973.
Schaie, K. R. Rigidity-flexibility and intelligence: a cross-sectional study of the adult life-span from 20 to 70. *Psychol. Monogr.* **72**: No. 462 (whole no. 9) (1958).
Schaie, K. W. Cross-sectional methods in the study of psychological aspects of aging. *J. Gerontol.* **14**:208–215 (1959).
Schaie, K. W. A general model for the study of developmental problems. *Psychol. Bull.* **64**:92–107 (1965).
Schaie, K. W. Age changes and age differences. *Gerontologist* **7**:128–132 (1967).
Schaie, K. W. A reinterpretation of age-related changes in cognitive structure and functioning. In L. R. Goulet and P. B. Baltes (eds.), *Life-span Developmental Psychology: Research and Theory.* New York: Academic Press, Inc., 1970.
Schaie, K. W. Can the longitudinal method be applied to studies of human development? In F. Z. Moenks, W. W. Hartup, and J. DeWitt (eds.), *Determinants of Behavioral Development.* New York: Academic Press, Inc., 1972.
Schaie, K. W. Methodological problems in description developmental research on adulthood and aging. In J. R. Nesselroade and H. W. Reese (eds.), *Life-span Developmental Psychology: Methodological Issues.* New York: Academic Press, Inc., 1973.
Schaie, K. W. Translations in gerontology—from lab to life: intellectual functioning. *Amer. Psychol.* **29**:802–807 (1974).
Schaie, K. W. Quasi-experimental designs in the psychology of aging. In J. E. Birren and K. W. Schaie (eds.), *Handbook of the Psychology of Aging.* New York: Van Nostrand Reinhold Co., 1977.

Schaie, K. W. Toward a stage theory of adult cognitive development. *J. Aging Human Develop.* **8**:129–138 (1977/78).
Schaie, K. W. External validity in the assessment of intellectual assessment in adulthood. *J. Gerontol.* **33**:695–701 (1978).
Schaie, K. W. The primary mental abilities in adulthood: an exploration in the development of psychometric intelligence. In P. B. Baltes and O. G. Brim, Jr. (eds.), *Life-span Development and Behavior*. Vol. 2. New York: Academic Press, Inc., 1979a, in press.
Schaie, K. W. Intelligence and problem solving. In J. E. Birren and R. B. Sloane (eds.), *Handbook on Mental Health and Aging*. Englewood Cliffs, New Jersey: Prentice-Hall, Inc., 1979b, in press.
Schaie, K. W., and Baltes, P. B. Some faith helps to see the forest: a final comment on the Horn and Donaldson myth on the Baltes-Schaie position on adult intelligence. *Amer. Psychol.* **32**:1118–1120 (1977).
Schaie, K. W., and Gribbin, K. Adult development and aging. *Ann. Rev. Psychol.* **26**:65–96 (1975a).
Schaie, K. W., and Gribbin, K. *The Impact of Environmental Complexity Upon Adult Cognitive Development*. Internat. Soc. Behav. Develop., Guildford, England, 1975b.
Schaie, K. W., Labouvie, G. V., and Barrett, T. J. Selective attrition effects in a fourteen-year study of adult intelligence. *J. Gerontol.* **28**:328–334 (1973).
Schaie, K. W., Labouvie, G. V., and Buech, B. U. Generational and cohort-specific differences in adult cognitive functioning: a fourteen-year study of independent samples. *Develop. Psychol.* **9**:151–166 (1973).
Schaie, K. W., and Labouvie-Vief, G. V. Generational versus ontogenetic components of change in adult cognitive behavior: a fourteen-year cross-sequential study. *Develop. Psychol.* **10**:305–320 (1974).
Schaie, K. W., and Marquette, B. W. Stages in transition: a bio-social analysis of adult behavior. Paper presented at the Satellite Meeting of the Internat. Soc. Human Develop., Kiryat Anavim, Israel, 1975.
Schaie, K. W., and Parham, I. A. *Manual for the Test of Behavioral Rigidity*. 2nd Edition. Palo Alto, Calif.: Consulting Psychologists Press, 1975.
Schaie, K. W., and Parham, I. A. Cohort-sequential analyses of adult intellectual development. *Develop. Psychol.* **13**:649–653 (1977).
Schaie, K. W., and Schaie, J. P. Intellectual development. In A. W. Chickering (ed.), *The Future American College*. San Francisco: Jossey-Bass, Inc., Publishers, 1979, in press.
Schaie, K. W., and Strother, C. R. The cross-sectional study of age changes in cognitive behavior. *Psychol. Bull.* **70**:671–680 (1968a).
Schaie, K. W., and Strother, C. R. The effects of time and cohort differences on the interpretation of age changes in cognitive behavior. *Multivar. Behav. Res.* **3**:259–293 (1968b).
Schaie, K. W., and Willis, S. L. Life-span development: implications for education. *Rev. Res. Educ.* (1978), in press.

Scheidt, R. J., and Schaie, K. W. A situational taxonomy for the elderly: generating situational criteria. *J. Gerontol.* **33**:848–857 (1978).
Spearman, C. E. *The Nature of Intelligence and the Principles of Cognition.* London: The Macmillan Co., 1927.
Storandt, M. Age ability level, and method of administering and scoring the WAIS. *J. Gerontol.* **32**:175–178 (1977).
Terman, L. M. *The Measurement of Intelligence.* Boston: Houghton Mifflin Co., 1916.
Thurstone, L. L. *Primary Mental Abilities.* Chicago: The University of Chicago Press, 1938.
Thurstone, L. L., and Thurstone, T. G. *Examiner Manual for the SRA Primary Mental Abilities Test.* Chicago: Science Research Associates, Inc., 1949.
Thurstone, T. G. *Manual for the SRA Primary Mental Abilities 11–17.* Chicago: Science Research Associates, Inc., 1958.
U.S. Public Health Service. *Eighth Revision International Classification of Disease, Adapted for Use in the United States.* USPHS Publ. No. 1693. Washington, D.C.: U.S. Government Printing Office, 1968.
Wechsler, D. *The Measurement of Adult Intelligence.* Baltimore: The Williams and Wilkins Co., 1939.
Welford, A. T. Motor performance. In J. E. Birren and K. W. Schaie (eds.), *Handbook of the Psychology of Aging.* New York: Van Nostrand Reinhold Co., 1977, pp. 450–496.
Wissler, C. *The Correlation of Mental and Physical Tests.* New York: Columbia University Press, 1901.
Yerkes, R. M. Psychological examining in the United States Army. *Memoirs Nat. Acad. Sci.* **15**:1–890 (1921).

5
Disease, Aging and Cognition: Relationships Between Essential Hypertension and Performance

Merrill F. Elias, Ph.D.

*Department of Psychology
University of Maine at Orono
Orono, Maine*

INTRODUCTION

Few investigators would disagree with the proposition that decline in cognitive ability and psychomotor performance with advancing age is sometimes an artifact of disease rather than a "natural" consequence of aging. It is not necessary to take sides with respect to the issue of whether or not aging is itself a disease process in order to accept the proposition that impaired physical health can influence performance and to take note of the fact that the incidence of impaired health increases with advancing age. In recent years, considerable attention has been focused on the adverse influence of disease on behavior (e.g., Abrahams, 1976; Elias, Elias, and Elias, 1977; Verwoerdt, 1976; Eisdorfer and Wilkie, 1977; Hertzog, Schaie, and Gribbin, 1978). However, as late as 1976, many investigators did not appear to recognize the implications of these findings for the control of health status in behavioral research on aging.

Table 5.1 summarizes findings relevant to health status in behavioral studies published in the *Journal of Gerontology* between 1963 and 1974.

Excluding the small percentage of studies that were directly con-

Table 5.1. Percentage of Studies Published in the *Journal of Gerontology* Between 1963 and 1968 and Between 1969 and 1974 That Reported or Reflected Concern for Health Status.*

	1963–1968	1969–1974
Studies concerned with health status	12.4%	10.4%
Studies controlling health status	17.1%	16.4%
Studies mentioning health status	41.9%	35.8%

* Adapted from Abrahams, Hoyer, Elias, and Bradigan. *J. Gerontol.* **30**:668–673 (1977). Reprinted with permission of the authors and editors.

cerned with health and behavior, only 16 to 17% of the studies reported any kind of control for health status. Further, the percentage of studies *not* mentioning health status of subjects increased from 28.6% in the first 5-year period to 37.3% in the second 5-year period. While these statistics are influenced by editorial decisions concerning general quality of manuscripts, and reflect studies published in only one journal concerned with aging, they are probably representative of the status afforded to the relevance of health factors to performance during the time period studied. A recent series of editorials and letters focusing on the need to screen human and animal subjects with regard to health status (Finch, 1977b; Levine, Bayat, and Rehman, 1977; Blumenthal, 1977) raises hope that health status will receive increasing attention in the next few years.

It is difficult to judge the influence of uncontrolled health status on specific studies. A report of health status for a stratified random probability sample of individuals residing in Durham County, North Carolina (Pfeiffer, 1973) provides some idea as to the incidence of disease in a sample of adults over 65 years of age. Twenty-five percent of the subjects in this sample suffered significant physical impairment. The percentage of physically impaired adults in age samples may be expected to vary depending on socioeconomic level, geographic area, and other demographic variables.

It is one thing to recognize the potentially confounding effects of disease processes on behavior; it is quite another to do something about it. The concern with regard to the practicality of screening human subjects for undesirable health characteristics is reflected in

Blumenthal's (1977) response to an editorial by Finch (1977a) and a letter from pathologists Levine, Bayat, and Rehman (1977): ". . . it is difficult to quarrel with the recommendation that each subject in an aging study be screened for disease. It's like being for motherhood. But the implementation of this ideal is generally more difficult than attaining motherhood (at least for normal females of appropriate age) . . . (Blumenthal, 1977)."

The exchange of editorials and letters was focused on autopsies and pathology studies in aging animals, but the point is well taken. Many psychologists have neither the expertise nor the necessary collaborative affiliations to undertake health-screening programs prior to behavioral testing. Insisting that this be done would severely limit the number of behavioral experiments which could be undertaken.

There may be reasonable compromises between the ignoring of health status completely and exhaustive medical examination. Self-report health inventories can be used for screening of subjects. For example, the Cornell Medical Index, a symptom checklist with questions related to systems (e.g., digestive, cardiovascular, vision, gastrointestinal), could be useful in this context. Wood, Elias, Schultz, and Pentz (1978) found that hypertensive subjects report more psychological and physical symptoms on the Cornell Medical Index than do normotensives. Botwinick and Storandt (1974) found that self-reported cardiovascular symptoms on the Cornell Medical Index were associated with slowing of reaction time regardless of age when two age groups (20-28, and 64-74 years) were compared. The inventory approach is not free from methodological problems. Some studies report age differences in accuracy and incidence of symptom reporting (see Brodman, Erdmann, Lorge, and Wolf, 1953; Desroaches, Kaiman, and Ballard, 1967; Monroe, Whiskin, Bonacich, and Jewell, 1965). Nevertheless, it provides more objective criteria for health assessment than general appearance and absence of spontaneous physical complaints. The reader who doubts that the latter criteria are employed has only to review manuscripts of studies on aging. It takes some amount of luck to make medical diagnosis on the basis of physical appearance, and it is not surprising to find that many subjects do not recite their medical history as a matter of course.

Our objective here is not to promote the use of medical inventories but rather to make the point that health status is not an insignificant issue, as some investigators imply. One other argument, advanced by those who shrink from the notion of screening for disease, is that exclusion of all but healthy subjects results in data which do not generalize to the population of older persons. This argument is easily challenged by pointing out that the investigator is not required to eliminate unhealthy subjects or to treat health status as an independent variable, but certainly there should be some obligation to describe the health characteristics of a sample, just as one would report years of education and gender.

There is little to be gained from a review of the many human and animal studies that provide examples of failure to control adequately for health status in studies on aging. It is more important to determine which diseases affect behavior, and to determine whether the effect is more pronounced for one age group than another. Obviously it is impossible to review all diseases. Many diseases (e.g., degenerating nervous-system diseases, severely debilitating stroke) have clear and unmistakable effects on behavior, and there is little question that they influence cognitive performance. It is the insidious diseases that represent the greatest potential for confounding in psychological studies, as their effects are not easily recognized via gross behavioral observation. Essential hypertension provides an excellent model for insidious disease, as neither the subject nor the investigator may be aware of its presence. Essential hypertension is thus the focus of this chapter, although several studies dealing with transient ischemic attacks, stroke, atherosclerosis, and disease-associated hypertension are reviewed. A distinction between essential (primary) hypertension and secondary hypertension is important to this discussion. The former represents hypertension in the absence of clinically recognizable pathology; the latter represents hypertension which is secondary to clinically identifiable diseases (e.g., renal disease, disease of the adrenal glands, and toxemia of pregnancy).

This chapter deals with the human literature, a literature which is largely descriptive in nature and beset by problems of sampling and control that characterize almost all applied clinical studies. The next chapter deals with genetically selected stocks as models for the study of hypertension, where the emphasis is on the advantages of the animal model in terms of control of variables that are impossible to control in human studies, and the problems and pitfalls which are peculiar to the use of animal models derived from genetic selection. These reviews are not exhaustive.[1] Major studies are reviewed with an emphasis on studies of hypertension in our laboratory.[2] (It may be useful to refer to the glossary of terms in Table 5.2.)

SPEED OF RESPONSE AND REACTION TIME

Spieth (1964, 1965) conducted one of the first comprehensive investigations of the relationship between cardiovascular disease and speed of response for middle-aged men (35–59 years). Two samples were used: (1) airline pilots and air traffic controllers who were referred to a Federal Aviation Authority medical clinic for a medical evaluation designed to determine physical fitness for certification, and (2) a smaller number of men who were not being examined in conjunction with certification. The subjects were divided into eight major groups described in Table 5.3. Presumably, subjects in groups IB, II, IIIA, and IVA were under a certain amount of stress induced by concern that they would not be certified for air traffic controller or pilot status because of their medical problems.

Subjects were given a ten-choice serial reaction-time task, the WAIS Symbol-Substitution Task, and the Trail-Making Test from the Halstead-Reitan Neuropsychological Test Battery. Scores from these tests were combined into a "composite" speed score. Subjects in categories IA and IB (healthy recruits and patients with unsubstantiated diagnoses) performed in a superior manner to subjects in all other groups, and this was true even when the age factor was controlled. There was one notable exception. Hypertensive subjects with blood pressures maintained at normal levels by medication (group IVB) performed as well as subjects in the healthy control group.

[1] A number of our reports on human studies are in various stages of preparation for publication, and we reserve the right to full exposition of our data. This work is the result of collaborative efforts involving Drs. Norman A. Schultz, Clyde A. Pentz, W. Gibson Wood, Kathleen C. Light, Wayne E. Watson, and Mr. John Dineen (all formerly of Syracuse University) and was done in collaboration with Dr. David H. P. Streeten's hypertension clinic at Upstate Medical Center, State University of New York, Syracuse. The studies were sponsored by a grant from the National Institute on Aging (AG 00868) to the author.

[2] After this chapter was prepared, Hertzog, Schaie, and Gribbin (1978) published the results of a statistical analysis of cross-sequential samples in order to explore the relationship between cardiovascular disease and test performance. This paper is well worth reading.

Table 5.2. Glossary of Some Terms Used in This Chapter.

Arteriosclerosis is a group of vascular diseases which are characterized by hardening, thickening, and loss of elasticity of the vessel walls.

Atherosclerosis is an occlusive disease that influences the nutrient vessels of the brain, heart, and kidneys by a progressive choking of the flow of blood. It is almost inevitably associated with advancing age, but may not be clinically significant if it does not interfere with blood flow in a significant manner.

Blood pressure (arterial blood pressure) is determined by the amount of blood that is pumped by the heart per unit of time and the diameter of the blood vessels.

Cerebrovascular accident is the technical name of a stroke. An ischemic stroke is defined as an interruption in cerebral blood flow which results in one or several neurological symptoms lasting for more than one day.

Diastolic blood pressure is the minimum pressure occurring during the relaxation phase of the cardiac cycle.

Essential hypertension is hypertension with no immediately identifiable pathology. It is very likely a common symptom of a number of disease processes.

Mean arterial pressure is ⅓ pulse pressure + diastolic pressure.

Normal blood pressure (normotensive) has never been precisely specified as it depends in part on statistical averages and clinical judgment as to what is not normal. A commonly accepted set of "average" values is 120 systolic and 80 diastolic, although 140/90 mm Hg, 145/90 mm Hg, and 150/95 mm Hg have been considered the upper limits of normal depending on an individual's age. Within the normal range of blood pressure, a sudden upward rise might be considered abnormal for a given individual.

Pulse pressure is the difference between systolic and diastolic blood pressure values.

Secondary hypertension is hypertension caused by a known disease process such as heart disease or renal insufficiency.

Systolic blood pressure is the maximum pressure occurring during the systolic (contraction) phase of the cardiac cycle.

Transient ischemic attack is a term reserved for ischemic stroke with symptoms that clear up after a day or seconds and may be associated with cell death.

The reason for the poorer performance in the nonmedicated hypertensive subjects relative to the medicated hypertensive subjects and the healthy controls was not readily apparent. Spieth postulated that some form of central nervous system pathology, related to cerebral blood flow, was responsible for the inferior performance of the hypertensive group. This group was potentially under greater stress at the time of testing than the normotensive and medicated hypertensive group; the latter two groups were not threatened with loss of certification to control air traffic or fly as a result of the medical examination. However, Spieth points out that the group of healthy subjects that thought they were diseased at the time of testing and faced the possi-

Table 5.3. Major Groups in Cardiovascular Disease–Speed Response Study.*

IA	Healthy recruits
IB	False positive referrals with diagnoses which were not substantiated at the clinic
II	Referrals and volunteers with mild or moderate congenital or rheumatic heart disorder
IIIA	Referrals who suffered from arteriosclerotic or coronary heart disease but were not hypertensive
IIIB	Volunteers with history and evidence of old myocardial infarction, coronary heart disease or arteriosclerosis without hypertension
IVA	Referrals with arterial hypertension which was not treated with drugs (blood pressure > 140/90 mm Hg)
IVB	Hypertensive recruits with blood pressure maintained within normal limits by medication
V	Individuals with a history or physical evidence of cerebrovascular disorder

NOTE: All subjects were middle-aged men, 35 to 59 years of age.
* Adapted from Spieth, 1964.

bility of not being certified (group IB) performed as well as the healthy subjects and the medicated hypertensive subjects.

While "differential stress" may not provide a satisfactory explanation of the differences between Spieth's medicated and nonmedicated hypertensive subjects, there was no direct evidence of impairment in cerebral blood flow for the hypertensive subjects or differences in cerebral blood flow between medicated and nonmedicated hypertensives. Thus, the question of why the medicated hypertensives performed better than the nonmedicated hypertensives remains unanswered.

In contrast to Spieth's study, superior performance for medicated hypertensive subjects relative to untreated hypertensive subjects was *not* observed in a study performed by K. C. Light (1975) at the Upstate Medical Center Hypertension Clinic (SUNY, Syracuse, New York). Her study deviated from Spieth's in several ways: (1) medicated and nonmedicated hypertensives (BP > 140/90 mm Hg) were tested in the context of a medical examination and were thus required to cease taking medication prior to testing; (2) medicated and nonmedicated hypertensives and some controls were tested under the influence of a potent diuretic that lowered blood pressure to normal or nearly normal levels; (3) results of the clinic's medical examination did not threaten future occupational status, at least not in the direct sense of certification. As may be seen in Table 5.4, the medicated hypertensives exhibited slower serial-discrimination reaction times than the untreated hypertensives, and performance for the nonmedicated hypertensives and normotensive controls did not differ. Consistent with findings by Spieth (1964), there was no significant age-by-blood pressure interaction. However, elderly subjects were not used in either study. The age range in Spieth's study was 35–59 years; the age range in Light's study was 18–59 years. Both investigators reported a slowing of serial-discrimination reaction time with advancing age.

Relatively poorer performance for Light's medicated hypertensive sample is not easily explained. Duration of hypertension was slightly greater for the medicated sample, but covariance adjustment for duration did not alter the results, and there was no significant regression of duration of hypertension on serial reaction-time scores. Response slowing occurred regardless of whether the medication employed could be classified as an arteriolar relaxer, a diuretic, or a general blocking agent of sympathetic nervous system activity. Furthermore, all subjects had been withdrawn from medication from 3 to 21 days prior to testing. Light offered some interesting speculations regarding

Table 5.4. **Means and Standard Deviations of Reaction-Time Scores on Tests of Serial Discrimination for Normotensive, Medicated Hypertensive, and Nonmedicated Hypertensive Subjects.***

Class	N		Age	2–Choice	3–Choice	8–Choice	Total RT
Normotensive	43	M	36.2	101.25	111.21	122.61	335.29
		SD	12.3	5.15	6.29	6.61	16.25
Nonmedicated hypertensive	42	M	38.1	103.82	113.10	124.35	341.26
		SD	10.7	6.43	7.51	7.29	19.88
Medicated hypertensive	118	M	43.0	111.46	120.63	132.80	355.84
		SD	10.7	36.69	32.24	30.93	25.29

NOTE: All RT measures are given in seconds.
* From: Light, K. C. *Exp. Aging Res.* 1:209–227 (1975). Reprinted with permission of the author and Beech Hill Enterprises, Inc. (formerly EAR, Inc.).

the poorer performance of medicated hypertensives. These speculations took into account the literature on cerebral blood flow and the possible relationships between autoregulatory mechanisms and the diuretic used during testing. However, as in Spieth's study, there was no direct physiological evidence that cerebral blood flow or any other physiological mechanism was responsible for the poorer performance of the medicated hypertensives.

Analysis of plasma renin activity (PRA) constitutes a central feature of hypertension research at the Upstate Medical Center Clinic (see Streeten, Schletter, Clift, Stevenson, and Dalakos, 1969), and thus Light was able to classify hypertensive patients into one of three PRA groups: low PRA, below 1.7 ng/ml/hr; normal PRA, 1.7–8.5 ng/ml/hr; and high PRA, above 8.5 ng/ml/hr. This subdivision of hypertensive subjects into PRA groups represented a recognition of the fact that essential hypertension does not represent a single disease entity, but rather multiple diseases with yet unknown etiologies. Renin analyses are particularly important to separation of samples of hypertensives on the basis of etiology. Renin is a hormone normally produced by the kidney when its perfusion is threatened by an abnormal reduction in blood pressure. It is not a pressor, but one of its products (angiotensin II) produces contraction at the arterioles which in turn increases vascular resistance and raises blood pressure. Angiotensin II also stimulates aldosterone secretion which acts on the kidney to increase retention of sodium ions and water, thus augmenting the fluid content of the circulatory system and elevating blood pressure (Marx, 1976).

It was once thought that perhaps a majority of hypertensives were victims of renin hypersecretion; however, most hypertensives ($\approx$ 57%) have normal PRA levels, and approximately 16% have high PRA levels (Marx, 1976). The importance of classification of hypertensives into PRA groups becomes apparent when one considers the prognostic significance of PRA. Light (1975) has summarized these findings:

> New evidence indicates that PRA level may be prognostically important for hypertensive patients. In one recent study (Brunner, Laragh, Baer, Newton, Goodwin, Krakoff, Bard, and Buhler, 1972), PRA was determined in 219 hypertensive subjects over a period of 4.5 years. Throughout this period, these subjects were treated with a variety of

antihypertensive agents. At the end of this period, the incidence of complications in low, normal and high PRA groups was compared. Brunner and his colleagues found that 11% of normal PRA subjects had suffered either cardiovascular or cerebrovascular infarcts. But, strikingly, none of the low PRA subjects has suffered infarction of any kind . . . (Light, 1975, p. 211).

Light reasoned that because PRA levels are prognostically important, one might expect to observe differences in serial reaction-time performance among persons classified on the basis of PRA levels.

Table 5.5 shows the results of the analysis of differences in total serial reaction time for the hypertensive subjects classified into the high, normal, and low PRA groups. There were too few subjects in the high PRA group to permit testing of the age-by-blood pressure interaction, but performance scores were adjusted for regression on age by means of covariance analysis. Medicated hypertensives exhibited slower reaction times than nonmedicated hypertensives for the low and normal PRA groups, but there were no differences between medicated and nonmedicated hypertensives for the high PRA group. For untreated hypertensive subjects, mean serial reaction times were

Table 5.5. Age-Adjusted Cell Means and Standard Deviations for the Interaction of Drug Treatment (Medication or No Medication) and the Results of Multiple Contrasts Between Means for Medicated (Treated) and Nonmedicated (Untreated) Hypertensive Subjects.*

	N		Total RT Treated	N		Total RT Untreated
Low renin	46	M	358.78	10	M	343.04
		SD	25.44		SD	13.52
Normal renin	59	M	352.09	28	M	342.91
		SD	24.78		SD	20.07
High renin	13	M	349.69	4	M	369.21
		SD	18.09		SD	23.27

NOTES: A line connecting values for means denotes a significant difference ($p < 0.01$). All RT measures are given in seconds.
* From: Light, K. C. *Exp. Aging Res.* 1:209–227 (1975). Reprinted with permission of the author and Beech Hill Enterprises, Inc. (formerly EAR, Inc.).

slowest for the subjects in the high PRA group. However, the unequal number of subjects in the three renin groups and the small number of subjects in the high renin groups may have (1) contributed to the PRA-by-medication interaction, and (2) a lack of power with respect to contrasts between medicated and nonmedicated hypertensives within the high renin group. The PRA-by-blood pressure interaction was *not* replicated ($p < 0.06$) in a second study by Light (1978), although the untreated high renin–hypertensives showed the slowest serial reaction times (see Figure 5.1). Again, the limited number of subjects available in the high renin groups may have been responsible for a lack of statistical power. Regardless of Light's findings, it seems important to classify subjects in terms of PRA level in behavioral experiments or, alternatively, to identify the number of subjects in a given sample with high, normal, and low PRA values. Further studies with larger numbers of subjects, grouped by PRA value, may reveal behavioral differences among the PRA groups. Unfortunately, it is difficult to obtain large numbers of high and low PRA subjects because the majority of hypertensives have normal PRA.

Difficulties involved in the interpretation of Spieth's and Light's findings illustrate some of the difficulties in making sense of the hypertension literature in terms of causal mechanisms. Both investigators

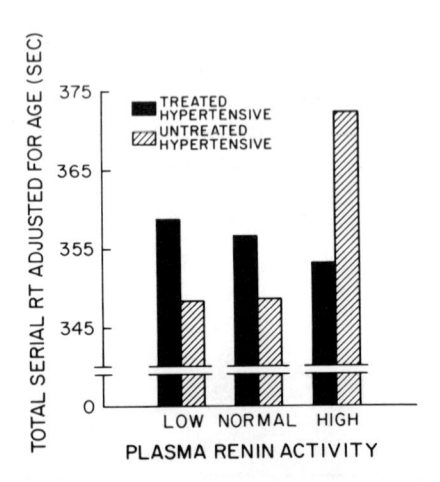

Figure 5.1. Total reaction time adjusted for age for treated and untreated hypertensive subjects with low, normal, and high plasma renin activity. [From: Light, K. C. *Exp. Aging Res.* **4**:3–22 (1978). Reprinted by permission of the author and Beech Hill Enterprises, Inc. (formerly EAR, Inc.)]

utilized hypertensives that were carefully screened for diseases secondary to hypertension or other medical problems, but neither could dictate the length of time that patients were medicated prior to testing. Duration of hypertension could not be established precisely, and effects of specific medications could not be separated. Duration of hypertension is always difficult to document. Subjects may have hypertension for an indeterminant time prior to detection and treatment. Retinopathy provides an indication of duration of hypertension, but it is not a direct indicator and does not discriminate among persons who may have mild elevations in blood pressure for unknown periods of time. It is not easy to separate drug effects, as different combinations of drugs are used on the same patient, and often the dosage of the drug is varied in an effort to obtain maximal control with minimal drug side effects. Further, there is always the possibility that drug treatment has been inappropriate.

The breakdown of hypertensive groups by etiology is important, but in many cases the etiology of essential hypertension is not known, and where it is known (e.g., high PRA), it is not always possible to find a sufficient number of patients free of secondary pathology to compare with low and normal PRA groups. These and other problems intrinsic to clinical research make it difficult to compare studies and, in our opinion, dictate a very cautious approach to convenient but undocumented explanations of the effects of blood pressure extremes on performance.

Very recently, Light (1978) completed a study which replicated her original findings and provided a comparison of hypertensive patients with patients suffering from cerebrovascular disease and mild heart disease. There were six categories of subjects in the study: (1) normotensive, (2) untreated hypertensive, (3) medicated hypertensive, (4) patients with coronary artery disease, (5) patients suffering transient ischemic attack (TIA), and (6) ischemic stroke patients. An ischemic stroke is generally defined as an interruption in cerebral blood flow which produces one or several neurological symptoms lasting for more than one day; for example, asymmetric weakness in the extremities, changes in reflexes, visual impairment, speech impairment, auditory impairment, memory impairment, and impairment in spatial functions. Light points out that symptoms lasting from a few seconds to a full day are defined as TIA's and may be associated with brain cell death. All of Light's TIA subjects were neurologically normal *at the time of testing.*

Three age groups of subjects were used (18–36, 37–55, and 56–77 years), although, as may be seen in Table 5.6, it was impossible to assign equal numbers of subjects to each diagnostic category under consideration. Hypertension was defined as systolic and diastolic blood pressures in excess of 140/90 mm Hg for the 18–36 and the 37–55-year-old subjects, and 150/90 mm Hg for the 60–77-year-old subjects. Testing was again accomplished in the hypertension screening clinic at Upstate Medical Center while patients were under the influence of a potent diuretic (furosemide).

As was true in Spieth's study, Light could not obtain enough subjects in each separate diagnostic category to test age-by-blood pressure interactions for each category of disease, and she did not obtain evidence for an age-by-vascular disease interaction when diagnostic categories were combined. Table 5.7 shows Light's findings for specific diagnostic groups with reaction times averaged over age. It is clear that some slowing in serial reaction time was observed for the TIA and stroke subjects in comparison to the patients with coronary heart disease and hypertension.

The normotensive subjects exhibited shorter reaction times than the treated hypertensive group, a finding consistent with Light's (1978) previous finding. Also consistent with Light's previous study, no dif-

Table 5.6. Distribution of Three Age Groups of Subjects in Diagnostic Groups of the Second Study By Light.*

VASCULAR STATUS	18–34	37–55	56–77	TOTAL
Normotensive	22	23	7	52
Untreated hypertensive	22	19	6	47
Treated hypertensive	30	74	26	130
Coronary heart disease	—	8	5	13
Transient ischemic attack	—	4	6	10
Stroke	—	9	10	19
Total	74	137	60	271

* From: Light, K. C. *Exp. Aging Res.* **4**:3–22 (1978). Reprinted with permission of the author and Beech Hill Enterprises, Inc. (formerly EAR, Inc.).

Table 5.7. Results of Light's Study of Reaction Time and Errors on a Serial-Discrimination Task.*

Class	N		2-Choice RT	3-Choice RT	8-Choice RT	Total RT	RT Errors
Normotensive	52	M	104.7	114.6	127.6	347.1	2.50
		SD	7.3	7.5	10.0	23.3	2.84
Untreated	47	M	107.6	117.0	128.0	352.7	2.27
hypertensive		SD	7.7	9.8	9.4	26.7	2.10
Treated	130	M	109.2	118.9	131.0	358.7	2.60
hypertensive		SD	9.2	9.8	9.8	26.5	2.61
Coronary heart	13	M	108.2	119.1	129.7	357.0	2.55
disease		SD	11.5	10.7	9.0	30.1	1.96
Transient	10	M	115.9	134.2	153.6	403.7	5.93
ischemic attack		SD	9.4	15.5	25.8	46.6	5.42
Stroke	19	M	111.4	127.9	144.7	382.4	3.98
		SD	13.2	17.7	18.1	44.1	3.42

NOTE: All timed measures are given in seconds.
* From: Light, K. C. *Exp. Aging Res.* **4**:3–22 (1978). Reprinted with permission of the author and Beech Hill Enterprises, Inc. (formerly EAR, Inc.).

ferences in serial reaction time were observed for the healthy normotensive controls and the nonmedicated (untreated) hypertensives. Patients with coronary heart disease did not differ from controls, but the two groups with *cerebrovascular* disorders (strokes and TIA's) differed significantly from the controls and the three groups with *cardiovascular* disorders. TIA and stroke patients did not differ significantly from each other. Serial reaction time increased with age, but there was no interaction of vascular status with age.

Table 5.8 summarizes findings for the type of medication used for the treated hypertensive subjects. There were no significant differences in serial reaction time for subjects on different types of medication, although too few persons were using tranquilizers alone to make this comparison meaningful. Of course drug dosages and previous drug history may influence performance. Usually, there is little that the investigator can do to control these variables. The possibility exists that hypertensive persons on medication had difficulty in adjusting to withdrawal from medication prior to clinic testing or that some unknown sample characteristic, for example, trait or state anxiety and/or depression (Friedman and Bennet, 1977), contributed to

Table 5.8. Relationship of General Category of Drug for the Treatment of Hypertension and Performance.*

	N		Total RT	Errors
Sympathetic inhibitor and other drug	72	M	357.0	2.6
		SD	23.3	2.9
Sympathetic inhibitor alone	17	M	362.0	3.2
		SD	24.8	2.2
Diuretic and vasodilator or tranquilizer	13	M	351.5	1.9
		SD	30.4	1.2
Diuretic or vasodilator alone	26	M	365.6	2.6
		SD	33.5	2.6
Tranquilizer alone	2	M	358.9	1.7
		SD	11.1	1.3

Note: All timed measures are given in seconds.
* From: Light, K. C. *Exp. Aging Res.* **4**:3–22 (1978). Reprinted with permission of the author and Beech Hill Enterprises, Inc. (formerly EAR, Inc.).

performance differences for the medicated and nonmedicated hypertensive subjects. In short, we have to fall back on speculation with regard to the differences between medicated and nonmedicated hypertensives, because control over dosage and appropriateness of previous drug treatment was not possible.

Before we leave the reaction-time data, it is important to note that mean differences in serial reaction time between normotensive and hypertensive subjects in the Spieth and Light studies are not of such a magnitude that would cause great concern with everyday tasks requiring discrimination and response. A plot of reaction time against blood pressure values by Light (1975) (see Figure 5.2) indicated more extreme performance scores for hypertensives and greater variation, but both normotensive and hypertensive subjects display considerable variation in reaction time. Small differences between means and individual differences within hypertensive and normotensive groups raise a question as to the practical or diagnostic significance of Spieth's and Light's findings. On the other hand, performance of tasks requiring extremely rapid response (e.g., pilot decision) might be affected in a significant manner, particularly when a sequence of tasks is performed and total accumulated time is important (see Table 5.4).

The general question of diagnostic or practical significance may

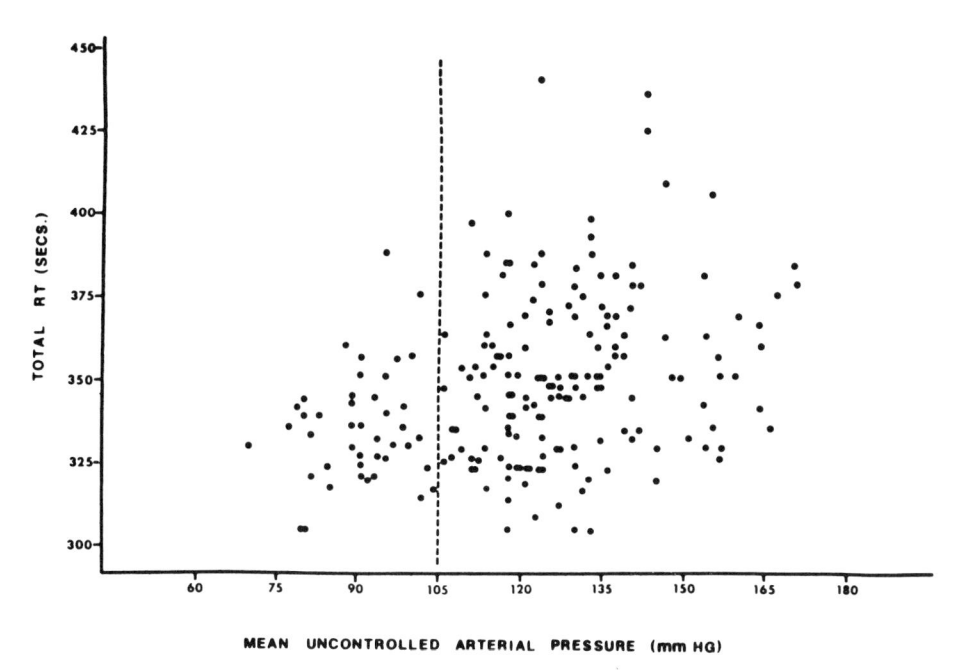

Figure 5.2. The relationship between total reaction time and uncontrolled blood pressure for the 203 subjects in Light's study ($r = 0.34$). A vertical dashed line separates normotensive and hypertensive subjects. [From: Light, K. C. *Exp. Aging Res.* **1**:209–228 (1975). Reprinted by permission of the author and Beech Hill Enterprises, Inc. (formerly EAR, Inc.)]

be best answered by considering the literature for tests commonly used in a diagnostic context, for example, the WAIS, the Wechsler Memory Scale, and the Halstead-Reitan Neuropsychological Test Battery.

WAIS PERFORMANCE

One of the most comprehensive studies of hypertension in relation to adult intelligence was done by Wilkie and Eisdorfer (1971). Subjects participating in a longitudinal study at Duke University were divided into two age groups *at initial testing* (60–69, and 70–79 years) and three blood pressure groups based on diastolic blood pressure values (normal, 66–95 mm Hg; borderline elevated, 95–105 mm Hg; hypertensive, 105 mm Hg and up). It is important to note that most of the subjects in the hypertensive group exhibited "end-organ changes," for example, retinopathy and cardiac thoracic ratios in excess of 50%. The borderline normotensive group exhibited significantly fewer end-organ changes. None of the subjects exhibited clinical evidence of cerebrovascular disease.

Figure 5.3 summarizes the major results of this study for the performance portion of the WAIS. The values reported are change scores; each subject was treated twice with a 10-year period between tests. The younger group of normotensive subjects (N) exhibited a rather minimal and nonsignificant decline in performance over the 10-year period. The older normotensives showed more decline over the 10-year period. The younger borderline hypertensive actually showed improvement over the 10-year period, but the older borderline hypertensives exhibited a decrement in performance. No data are shown for the older hypertensive group (H) because none of these subjects

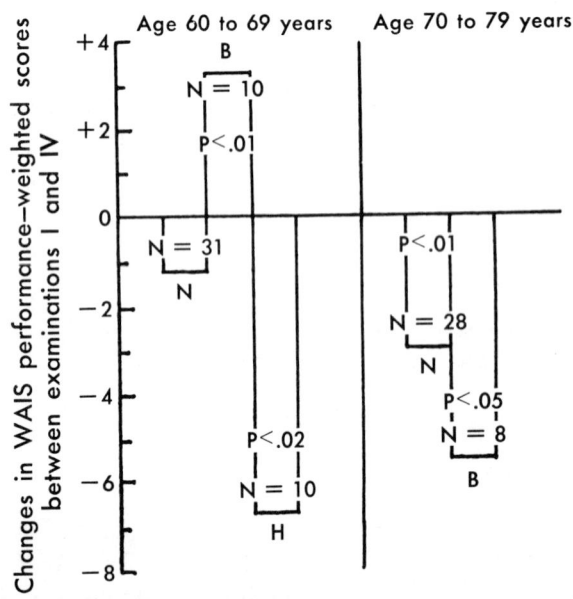

Figure 5.3. Changes in WAIS performance scores over a 10-year period for two different age groups of subjects with normal (N), borderline elevated (B), and hypertension (H). [From: Wilkie, F., and Eisdorfer, C. *Science* **172**:959–962 (1971). Copyright 1971 by the American Association for the Advancement of Science. Reprinted by permission.]

returned 10 years later for the follow-up testing necessary to derive change scores. Some subjects in the 60–69-year-old group also failed to return for testing. For both the 70–79 and the 60–69-year-old age groups, subjects that failed to return for the second test exhibited the lowest initial WAIS scores. Some significant correlations between the Verbal subscale scores and blood pressure values were obtained, but the major findings of impaired performance for hypertensives and the older borderline group were obtained on the Performance portion of the WAIS. It is clear that the change over the first 10-year period of observation was greatest for the group with the highest incidence of hypertension-related pathology. For the second 10-year period, the subjects with borderline blood pressure values exhibited a significant decline in performance which was of greater magnitude than that observed for normotensive subjects.

The most interesting finding was the improvement in performance for the first 10-year period of observation for the normotensive subjects. Citing studies of cerebral blood flow by Obrist (1964), Wilkie and Eisdorfer suggested that borderline elevations in blood pressure may have been beneficial to 60–69-year-old subjects because mild elevations in blood pressure may be necessary to maintain adequate cerebral blood flow. However, the study was not designed to test the blood-flow hypothesis.

Wilkie and Eisdorfer's data illustrate the potential age bias that could result if investigators inadvertently included samples of hypertensive patients in investigations which are intended to characterize changes in intellectual functioning for adults over 60 years of age. However, the study did not identify a specific pathology or pathologies responsible for decrements observed for the hypertensive patient, and it was not possible to separate effects of medication from effects of hypertension. One cannot withold treatment from patients; thus, many were on medication. Dose and type of medication varied from patient to patient.

Two of the very important differences between the Wilkie and Eisdorfer study and the studies by Spieth and Light were as follows: Wilkie and Eisdorfer's subjects were elderly, and many exhibited hypertension-related pathologies. Recent studies in our laboratory (Schultz, Dineen, Elias, Pentz, and Wood, in press) provide data on the WAIS for essential hypertensives (free from hypertension-associated pathology) who were similar in age to Light's sample of hypertensives. The WAIS was administered to two adult age groups (21–39, and 45–65 years) under exactly the same conditions and with the same population of clinic patients employed by Light in her serial reaction-time studies (Light, 1975, 1978). We were interested in whether Light's findings of poorer performance for medicated than nonmedicated hypertensives and controls would be replicated with a test more reflective of general intellective functioning, and whether the absence of age-by-blood pressure interactions characterizing Spieth's (1964, 1965) and Light's (1975, 1978) studies would be observed in a study with the WAIS. Consistent with Light's procedure, subjects with angina pectoris, congestive heart failure, history of kidney transplant, improper use of medication, type II or III eye-ground changes, neurological disorder, cerebrovascular accident, and myocardial infarction were eliminated from the sample. Less than 10% of the subjects in the sample had cholesterol levels that exceeded 260 mg/100ml and only one was below 120 mg/100ml.

Table 5.9 summarizes blood pressure values, age level, and years of education for the hypertensive and normotensive subjects. Preliminary analyses of WAIS scores revealed no differences between patients that were on medication prior to testing and those that had never been on medication. WAIS scores of normotensive controls that did not go through the medical screening procedure and those of medically examined controls did not differ significantly. Therefore these groups were combined, and a single group of hypertensives was compared with a single group of controls. Sex did not interact significantly with any other factor. It may be seen (Table 5.9) that education level was fairly well equated for these groups.

Hypertension was found to be negatively associated with WAIS Verbal scaled scores for the younger but not for the older subjects. When WAIS Performance scores were analyzed for subjects matched on WAIS Verbal scores (Table 5.10), a significant age-by-blood pressure interaction was found. Differences between hypertensive and normotensive subjects were greater for the younger than for the older group. We did not obtain any significant differences between groups of subjects with high, low, and normal plasma renin activity. Age differences in performance were observed only for the normotensive subjects.

Table 5.9. Means and Standard Deviations for Hypertensive and Normotensive Subjects in a Study Conducted at Syracuse University.*

		Systolic	Diastolic	Age	Education
Younger normotensive	($n = 22$)	115(13.10)	71(6.70)	26.20(4.80)	15.95(1.95)
Older normotensive	($n = 20$)	122(12.10)	72(7.50)	55.55(7.20)	15.50(1.70)
Younger hypertensive	($n = 31$)	150(13.25)	98(10.35)	29.70(5.35)	14.45(2.50)
Older hypertensive	($n = 37$)	161(16.95)	104(12.80)	52.40(4.90)	13.90(2.70)

* From: Schultz, N. R., Dineen, J. T., Elias, M. F. et al. *J. Gerontol.* **34**:246–253 (1979); reprinted with permission.

Analyses for specific performance subtests indicated no age-by-blood pressure interaction. Young subjects performed better than older adults on the Block Design subtest. High blood pressure subjects performed less well than normotensive subjects on Digit Symbol, Block Design, Picture Arrangement, and Object Assembly.

Findings of poorer performance for hypertensive subjects are generally consistent with findings by Wilkie and Eisdorfer (1971) for their older sample of adults (60–70, 70–80 years). Findings of more exaggerated effects of hypertension on performance scores for older than for younger subjects in Wilkie and Eisdorfer's (1971) study and more exaggerated effects of hypertension for the younger adults in our WAIS study are not at all inconsistent, although they may appear

Table 5.10. WAIS Performance Scores for Normotensive and Hypertensive Subjects Matched on WAIS Verbal Scaled Scores.*

Age Group	Normotensive Scaled Score	Hypertensive Scaled Score
Younger	69.9(4.7)$n = 15$	55.5(9.2)$n = 15$
Older	61.8(7.7)$n = 15$	55.9(5.1)$n = 15$

* From: Schultz, N. R., Dineen, J. T., Elias, M. F. et al. *J. Gerontol.* **34**:246–253 (1979); reprinted with permission.

to be. The two studies are not directly comparable. Wilkie and Eisdorfer's subjects were older than ours, and many exhibited pathological changes characteristic of sustained hypertension. They used a longitudinal design; ours was cross-sectional.

Our cross-sectional data indicated that hypertension can bias performance in the direction of poorer performance for *younger* adults. The reasons are not clear. Blood pressure elevations were greater for the older subjects. Unknown differences in sampling characteristics of young and older groups may be responsible for the interaction observed, perhaps as a result of some form of selective dropout of potentially poorer performing hypertensive subjects. Wilkie, Eisdorfer, and Nowlin (1976) have suggested that anxiety may explain the poorer performance of hypertensive subjects on some tasks. Wood, Elias, Schultz, and Pentz (1979) have reported higher state anxiety scores and Zung depression scores for the younger hypertensive subjects than for younger normotensive subjects (mean age = 25). This relationship was not observed for older normotensives and hypertensives (mean age = 54). However, differences were small in an absolute sense, and regressions of anxiety and depression scores on WAIS scores (Wood et al., unpublished) were not significant.

While hypertensives in our study performed less well than normotensives, the absolute magnitude of the differences were *not* such that one could make a case for their clinical-diagnostic significance or express concern for the ability of essential hypertensives to meet the everyday demands on cognitive functioning. The level of performance for these relatively well-educated hypertensive subjects exceeded that of the average score for the normative WAIS sample.

A question can be raised as to whether tests more specifically designed to permit inferences with regard to adequacy of cognitive functioning in relationship to brain functioning would reveal impairments of practical importance. Studies of performance on tests from the Halstead-Reitan battery (Reitan and Davidson, 1974) are relevant to this question.

HALSTEAD-REITAN TESTS

Table 5.11 provides a brief description of some of the various tests in the Halstead-Reitan Neuropsychological Battery. Some of the tests,

Table 5.11. Brief Summaries of the Content of the Neuropsychological Tests Used in Our Studies of Essential Hypertension.*

Category Test. The Category Test is the most sensitive test of brain impairment in the Halstead-Reitan battery. It involves abstraction concept formation and the ability to form learning sets. Subjects are presented with stimulus figures. After viewing a set of four figures, the subject is asked to indicate which of the four figures is "correct." Correctness is based on stimulus dimensions which change through the series of presentations. The total number of errors on the test is recorded.

Tactual Performance Test (TPT)–Time Component. This test measures ability to adapt to a novel problem-solving situation and to perform a tactual-sensory motor task without the aid of visual cues. The subject is blindfolded and instructed to fit wooden blocks of different common geometric shapes into a formboard. The task is performed first with the preferred hand, next with the nonpreferred hand, and finally with both hands. The sum of these three scores is used as a time score. (In clinical settings, times required to complete the task with the right, left, and both hands are compared.)

TPT–Memory Component. This test measures ability to recall spatial relationships. After the subject completes the timed portion of the TPT (see above), the formboard is removed from sight and the blindfold is removed. The subject is then required to draw the forms of the blocks that were placed in the formboard (but not seen). The score is the number of shapes correctly reproduced. The score is determined by whether or not the shape was correctly recalled, rather than the accuracy of the drawing per se.

TPT–Localization Component. This portion of the TPT measures the ability to remember spatial relationships. When the subject is instructed to draw the blocks for the TPT–Memory Test, he is also asked to place the blocks in their correct relationships with respect to their relationships on the formboard. The score is the number of shapes that are drawn in their correct position.

Finger Oscillation (Finger Tapping) Test. This test measures speed of tapping with the index finger. A special key arrangement records the number of taps. The mean of five consecutive 10-second finger taps (within five of each other) is computed for the preferred hand and the nonpreferred hand. (In clinical practice, performances for the dominant and nondominant hands are compared.)

Trail-Making Tests (Parts A and B). These tests measure the subject's ability to scan visual materials and to perform sequential behaviors under time constraints. Circled letters or numbers are arranged in a scattered manner on a sheet of paper. There are two parts to the test. For Part A, the stimuli are circled numbers, and the subject is instructed to draw lines to connect the numbers in order. For Part B, the stimuli are circles containing numbers or letters. The subject is instructed to draw lines from numbers to letters in an alternating numerical-alphabetical sequence. The time to complete each test is recorded as well as the number of errors made in connecting the circles. (In clinical practice, performance for letters versus performance for letters and numbers are compared.)

Table 5.11. (continued)

Impairment Index. This index provides a summary of scores on the battery that fall in the brain-damaged range based on cutting scores established by Halstead and Reitan. The Impairment Index indicates the proportion of tests failed. It ranges from 0 to 1.0. Scores of 0.5 and above are generally considered in the brain-damaged range. The index is normally calculated on the basis of 10 scores but a prorated score can be obtained for five tests.

NOTE: These are only some of the many tests employed by Halstead and Reitan (see Reitan and Davidson, 1974).
* From D. Klisz in *The Clinical Psychology of Aging.* Reprinted by permission.

such as the Tapping (finger oscillation) Test, are performed with the dominant and nondominant hands and afford an opportunity for the investigator to compare performance for right and left sides of the body. Often, significant "asymmetries" in performance are indicative of impairment in the contralateral cerebral hemisphere. Some tests in the battery are performed poorly by subjects with damage in the right versus the left cerebral hemisphere and vice versa. All of the tests discriminate between brain-damaged and non-brain-damaged subjects, but they become a maximally effective diagnostic tool when used together. When five or more tests are used, an impairment index can be calculated: number of tests performed in brain-damage range/number of tests given. A score of 0 reflects no impairment. A score of 1 reflects maximal impairment. Using Halstead-Reitan cutting scores, an impairment index of 0.5 or above is presumed to indicate brain damage.

In addition to the serial reaction-time measures discussed previously, Spieth (1964, 1965) administered the Halstead Tactual Performance Test and the WAIS Block Design subtest. The Tactual Performance Test (TPT) is particularly sensitive to brain damage in general and involves a memory score as well as a "form-placement score" for both dominant and nondominant hands (Reitan and Davidson, 1974). In Spieth's study several scores were derived from the TPT: total time to complete the task three times, time on the third trial, and number of shapes and locations correctly produced in an untimed recall test. The subjects with cerebrovascular disease (see Table 5.3) performed at a lower level than healthy subjects on all measures. Medicated hypertensive subjects and subjects with rheumatic-congenital heart disease did not differ significantly from healthy controls. Subjects with somatic arteriosclerotic or coronary heart disease of a moderate nature, a history and evidence of old myocardial infarctions, coronary heart disease, or arteriosclerosis without hypertension, hypertension, and hypertensive cardiovascular disease in mild or moderate form were combined into a single group and compared with the healthy group. This enabled age comparisons to be made with adequate numbers of subjects. In general, the combined pathology group performed less well than the healthy control group in all TPT measures except for recall of block locations. No age-by-vascular status interaction was observed when five age groups were compared: 35–39, 40–44, 45–49, 50–54, and 55–59 years. However, time required to complete the TPT increased with increasing age.

For the modified Block Design subtest of the WAIS, the combined cardiovascular pathology group (IIIA, IIIB, and IVA, Table 5.3) performed more slowly than the healthy controls, and older subjects required significantly fewer block shapes and locations than younger subjects for healthy and nonhealthy groups. It is important to note that (1) Spieth's groups were above-average educationally, and (2) the performance of subjects in the cardiovascular pathology group, although statistically different from that of the control group, was 1 standard deviation above that observed for the normative WAIS sample.

Spieth's results were in general agreement with previous studies of middle-aged individuals with coronary heart disease and hypertension. Enzer, Simonson, and Blankstein (1942) reported that subjects with coronary heart disease and/or hypertension exhibited a lower maximum finger-tapping rate than healthy controls. Apter, Halstead, and Heimburger (1951) found that essential hypertensive subjects exhibited significantly higher indexes of organic brain impairment than controls when the Halstead Impairment Index was used as a criterion score.

More recently, Goldman and co-workers (1974) administered the Halstead-Reitan Category Test to 14 relatively poorly educated (mean = 9.3 years; SD = 3.6) male subjects (mean age = 48 years; SD = 14.5) with very high blood pressure (mean systolic/diastolic =

173/118 mm Hg). The Category Test is a particularly sensitive test of brain impairment. The subject must attend to relevant stimuli, ignore irrelevant stimuli, and make discriminations among stimuli under circumstances where the relevant dimension shifts periodically. In general, it is a test of learning-set formation and problem solving. The mean error scores for the hypertensive patients were in an absolute range suggestive of cerebral impairment. Error scores correlated positively with diastolic blood pressures with ($r = 0.52$). Essentially the same results were obtained when scores were adjusted statistically for age (adjusted $r = 0.48$) and IQ (adjusted $r = 0.57$).

Goldman and co-workers did not compare hypertensives with controls, and they used only a single age group. We (Pentz et al., in press) compared younger (21–35 years) and older (45–65 years) hypertensives with normotensive controls. Based on previous findings of poorer performance by older than by younger subjects on the tests (see Klisz, 1978, for a review), we hypothesized an age-by-blood pressure interaction with more pronounced differences between hypertensives and controls for the older than for the younger subjects (we had not yet analyzed the WAIS data). All subjects had participated in WAIS testing at Upstate Medical Center and were carefully screened with the same medical diagnostic procedures. They were given several tests from the Halstead-Reitan battery (Trail Making, Tapping, Category, and the Tactual Performance Test) as well as measures of depression and state and trait anxiety. As in the studies by Light (1975, 1978) and our studies with the WAIS (Schultz et al., in press), some hypertensive subjects were on medication at the time of testing and some were not. An important difference was that our subjects were not under the influence of a diuretic during testing.

As in our study with the WAIS, no differences were observed among high, low, and normal plasma renin activity subjects for any of the neuropsychological tests. Older subjects generally performed less well than younger subjects on the speed and localization portions of the Tactual Performance Test (TPT) and the Trail-Making A test. This finding was consistent with previous findings for these tests (see Klisz, 1978). Hypertensive subjects performed less well than normotensive subjects on the Category Test and on the memory portion of the Tactual Performance Test. There were no significant main effects or interactions for the Impairment Index.

There was a blood pressure-by-age interaction for the TPT-memory test, but the nature of the interaction was in opposition to our hypothesis. The difference in performance between hypertensive and normotensive subjects was more exaggerated for the *younger* subjects. Impaired performance on a memory test for hypertensives has been reported by Wilkie, Eisdorfer, and Nowlin (1976). Initial performance for hypertensives and normotensives was similar, but hypertensives exhibited significant loss on an immediate recall task of the Logical Memory Test and the Visual Reproduction Test when they were retested after 6.5 years. Wilkie and co-workers (1976) speculated that these findings may have reflected difficulty in dealing with changes in set or state anxiety associated with the testing situation. Our (Pentz et al., in press) younger hypertensive subjects exhibited higher state anxiety and depression scores than all other groups. However, none of the scores were in the clinically significant range in terms of test norms, and the regressions of anxiety and depression scores on the neuropsychological test scores were not significant. Thus anxiety and depression, as measured in our study, do not provide an explanation of the poorer performance of the young hypertensive subjects.

Examination of scatter plots for the neuropsychological tests indicated considerable variation in performance within normotensive and hypertensive groups. Assignment of subjects to hypertensive and normotensive groups on the basis of brain-damage cutoff scores (see Reitan and Davidson, 1974) resulted in an unacceptable number of false positive (brain-damage score–normotensive) and false negative predictions (normal score–hypertensive). Despite the fact that prediction of hypertensive status on an individual basis was poor, the findings demonstrate that age bias introduced by hypertension can result in lower performance scores for *younger* subjects.

Our findings for the neuropsychological tests reflect a cohort effect rather than an age effect, as we employed a cross-sectional design. However, very recently, Hertzog, Schaie, and Gribbin (1978) reported an *increment* in performance on several subtests of the Primary Mental Abilities Test (PMA) (Thurstone and Thurstone, 1949) for essential hypertensive subjects tested at 56 years of age and again 7 years later; Spatial, Number, and Intellectual Ability scores showed improvement between 56 and 63 years of age, but Psychomotor Speed showed decline. Subjects with cerebrovascular disease, hypertension with atherosclerosis, and atherosclerosis showed a decline on the Spatial Abilities, Intellectual Ability and Psychomotor Speed tests. Hertzog and co-workers point out that this difference in findings between their study and the Wilkie and Eisdorfer (1971) longitudinal study with hypertensive subjects, may be due to hypertension-related pathologies in Wilkie and Eisdorfer's hypertensive group. The Wilkie and Eisdorfer *borderline* hypertensives showed an *improvement* in performance over their 10-year test-retest period. These subjects were probably most directly comparable to the essential hypertensive subjects of Hertzog and co-workers and to our subjects.

PSYCHOMOTOR PERFORMANCE IN HEALTHY SUBJECTS

While "healthy controls" are a necessary reference group in studies of cardiovascular disease and behavior, the performance of healthy subjects of differing ages is of interest in its own right, because it speaks directly to the question of whether performance decrements with advancing age occur in subjects that are free from disease.

Szafran (1963, 1965, 1966a, 1966b, 1968) conducted behavioral investigations with subjects that may be characterized as suprahealthy; that is, active duty pilots (20 to 60 years of age) who were subjected to exhaustive medical screening prior to comprehensive behavioral testing. Behavioral testing included a variety of tasks involving discrimination and rapid decision making under varying amounts of task difficulty and sensory-perceptual load. Szafran's findings indicated no age-associated differences in performance even under very demanding overload conditions. He postulated that those studies which do reveal slowing of psychomotor response with advancing age may have inadvertently included subjects with covert or "subclinical" cardiovascular disorders.

Szafran's interesting speculation and his data are often cited as evidence that cardiovascular disease has an adverse effect on performance. However, decline in performance has been observed in a number of studies in which medical screening of healthy subjects has been accomplished (e.g., Spieth, 1964, 1965; Abrahams and Birren, 1973; Light, 1975, 1978; Schultz et al., in press; Pentz et al., in press). Szafran's subjects seem to have been screened more thoroughly than subjects in other studies. Also, pilots represent a highly practiced sample with regard to decision making and serial-psychomotor responding under conditions where perceptual load is high and there are demands on rapid response. Selective dropout of poor performers is undoubtedly an important performance-determining factor for a pilot sample, as those who do not have the requisite performance skills either do not stay in the profession or do not live to an old age. The most conservative conclusion based on Szafran's data is that not all older persons show decline with advancing age and that occupation and a variety of occupational correlates such as practice and health status play an important role in age-associated characteristics.

The issue of age changes and good health has received much more attention than can be given here. The reader may wish to consult papers on terminal drop (e.g., Siegler, 1975).

NEGATIVE FINDINGS

The notion of ill health, particularly cardiovascular disease, has received so much attention in the last several years that studies with negative findings have received somewhat less attention than they deserve. Thompson, Eisdorfer, and Estes (1970) found that an association between impaired WAIS performance and cardiovascular disorders was no longer significant after socioeconomic level and race were taken into account. Only 39% of the higher socioeconomic subjects were diseased as opposed to 67% of the subjects in lower socioeconomic groups. These data do not imply that cardiovascular diseases do not represent a potentially confounding variable with respect to examination of age-related trends in behavior. Rather, they suggest that studies of cardiovascular-behavioral relationships must control for socioeconomic status as much as possible within the constraints of data collection.

Another study with negative findings was reported by Hertzog, Gribbin, and Schaie (1975). The Primary Mental Abilities Test was used to assess the cognitive performance of 150 subjects over a period of 17 years. Initially, the investigators found no effects on performance which could be related to cardiovascular disease. After better controls were introduced for type of disease, severity of onset, and type of pathology, a decline in test performance was associated with cardiovascular pathology.

Abrahams (1976) calls attention to a very important characteristic of studies in which the effects of cardiovascular disease have either not been observed or have been minimal. Their subjects received repeated health assessments through the years. Therefore, they were not only more concerned about their health, but were more likely to have had their cardiovascular disease diagnosed and treated prior to a time that it became serious enough to interfere with cognitive performance.

CEREBRAL BLOOD FLOW

Cerebral blood flow is probably the most frequently singled out physiological phenomenon with respect to hypotheses regarding impaired performance for persons with hypertension diseases. Light (1975, 1978) discussed cerebral blood flow in the context of her finding that medicated hypertensives performed better than untreated hypertensives; Spieth (1964, 1965) speculated with regard to cerebral blood flow in the context of his finding that untreated hypertensives performed less well than medicated hypertensives and controls. While these hypotheses have not been tested directly, there is evidence that cerebral blood flow is altered by various forms of vascular disease, and that cerebral blood flow influences performance (e.g., Obrist and Busse, 1965; Obrist, 1964; Obrist and Bissell, 1955).

Earlier, we took note of Wilkie and Eisdorfer's (1971) hypothesis that borderline elevated blood pressure levels might be beneficial to the maintenance of cerebral circulation and consequently the maintenance of cognitive abilities. There is some indirect evidence for this hypothesis, as Obrist, Busse, and Henry (1961) found that low blood pressure was associated with more diffuse EEG slowing than mildly elevated blood pressure in a group of elderly psychiatric patients. While there have been studies of blood flow and behavior in subjects who have suffered cerebrovascular accidents, transient ischemic attacks and subjects with atherosclerosis, there have been few, if any, systematic studies of the relationship of abnormal variations in blood pressure on blood flow in relationship to cognitive performance for different age groups of subjects. Until such studies are accomplished, it would seem that conservatism regarding the role of blood flow in the poorer performance of essential hypertensive patients is in order. Most of the studies of essential hypertension have not been able to control nonphysiological variables that may explain performance differences between hypertensive and normotensive subjects.

SUMMARY, CONCLUSIONS, AND FUTURE DIRECTIONS

More serious forms of vascular disease (e.g., cerebrovascular disease, severe atherosclerosis, hypertension accompanied by other kinds of vascular disorders) are associated with performance decrements on cognitive tasks. The situation is less clear with respect to essential hypertension. Hypertensives usually perform less well than normotensives, even under circumstances where highly educated subjects have been carefully screened for medical problems other than hypertension. Several cross-sectional studies of WAIS performance and neuropsychological test performance indicate that differences between hypertensive and normotensive subjects are more pronounced for younger than for older adults when all subjects are less than 65 years of age. One study of changes in performance over a 7-year period indicates that essential hypertensives exhibit an increment in performance scores on some tests of cognitive ability, although a decline in performance was observed for a test measuring psychomotor speed. Thus, age bias introduced by the presence of essential hypertensives in studies on aging may not always favor better performance for younger subjects. It depends on the ages of the age groups compared, the type of task, and on whether subjects are malignant hypertensives or essential hypertensives.

While age-by-blood pressure interactions dictate experimental designs which take into consideration the presence of essential hypertensives in cross-sectional and longitudinal studies, differences in performance are often not of a magnitude that should cause concern with regard to everyday functioning. Individual differences are large for both normotensive and hypertensive subjects, and the clinical prediction of hypertensive and normotensive status, on the basis of neuropsychological and WAIS test scores, is poor. While well-educated hypertensive subjects perform less well than well-educated normotensive subjects on the WAIS, they perform substantially above the mean for the WAIS sample.

We do not yet understand why essential hypertensive subjects exhibit lower scores than normotensive samples on some cognitive tasks. Two kinds of explanations have been popular: (1) speculations about alterations in cerebral blood flow and (2) speculations about the presence of pathological changes that are present, but not recognizable, on the basis of clinical diagnostic evaluation. These speculations are not unreasonable in terms of present knowledge concerning the effects of hypertension on the nervous system, but the studies that spawned them offer no direct evidence that essential hypertension is linked to impaired performance via the mechanisms of cerebral blood flow or "subclinical pathology." In fact, a causal relationship between essential hypertension and impaired cognitive performance has not been established.

It is difficult to eliminate the potential contribution of nonphysiological factors that may influence the sampling characteristics of younger and older hypertensives. Studies in our laboratory indicate that effects of anxiety and depression on performance do not provide an explanation of the poorer performance of hypertensive subjects, but these, and other noncognitive factors, deserve further investigation.

One study has indicated that medicated hypertensive subjects perform less well than nonmedicated hypertensives and controls, while another has indicated that nonmedicated hypertensives perform less well than medicated hypertensives and controls. Several studies indicate no differences between medicated hypertensives and controls. These discrepant findings are difficult to resolve either because the methodologies have been substantially different, or the performance tests have been different. Where medicated hypertensives have performed less well than normotensives, estimated duration of hypertension and category of drug action did appear to explain the findings, but adequate control of dosage and duration of treatment with medication was not possible, and duration of hypertension could not be determined precisely.

Two important directions for future studies are: (1) identification of nonphysiological and noncognitive factors that may be influencing age-by-blood pressure interactions and (2) the development of improved paper-and-pencil screening techniques for the identification of subjects with vascular disease. It is not practicable for investigators to perform physical examinations on subjects in the normal course of experimentation. Investigators should be encouraged to describe the health status of their subjects in general terms and to conduct more systematic screening for health status than is presently the case.

Recent studies have separated subjects into distinct groups with regard to specific type of vascular pathology. This represents a recognition of the fact that it is now time to ask what kinds of diseases influence specific behaviors. The same strategy needs to be employed in studies of hypertension and cognitive behavior, as it is now recognized that even essential hypertension does not have a single etiology. Classification of subjects in terms of plasma renin activity represents a recognition of this fact.

While it is recognized that placing subjects with subtypes of vascular disease into a single group is like adding apples and oranges, it is no simple matter to obtain the numbers of subjects required for adequate statistical power for the testing of age-by-disease interactions. One solution is to perform more intensive longitudinal studies, even if only for short time segments. Longitudinal studies are not free of methodological problems. Individuals who live long enough to permit collection of longitudinal data may not be representative of all persons with vascular disease (see Hertzog et al., 1978). However, longitudinal studies over segments of time would be of value, particularly with respect to essential hypertensives, as they tend to remain in longitudinal studies (Hertzog et al., 1978). Those subjects that do develop malignant forms of hypertension during the study should not be discarded from the longitudinal samples. They should be compared with those subjects who do not develop malignant hypertension. Retrospective comparisons for these two groups would be of considerable value; that is, comparisons when they were both essential hypertensive.

No matter how elegant the design, there are countless life-history variables that simply cannot be equated for normotensive and hypertensive subjects. It is for this reason that some investigators have turned to animal models for hypertension. The rationale for using animal models is relatively simple, and the opportunity for control of drugs, treatment, and duration of hypertension is seductive. But, as we shall see in the next chapter, animal studies are not free from methodological problems.

REFERENCES

Abrahams, J. P. Psychological correlates of cardiovascular diseases. In M. F. Elias and B. E. Eleftheriou (eds.), *Special Review of Experimental Aging Research: Progress in Biology*. Bar Harbor, Maine: EAR, Inc., 1976, pp. 330–350.

Abrahams, J. P., and Birren, J. E. Reaction time as a function of age and behavioral predisposition to coronary heart disease. *J. Gerontol.* **28**:471–478 (1973).

Abrahams, J. P., Hoyer, W. J., Elias, M. F., and Bradigan, B. Gerontological research in psychology published in the *Journal of Gerontology* 1963–1974: perspectives and progress. *J. Gerontol.* **30**:668–673 (1975).

Apter, N. S., Halstead, C. W., and Heimburger, R. F. Impaired cerebral functions in essential hypertension. *Am. J. Psych.* **107**:808–813 (1951).

Blumenthal, H. T. Letters to the editor: some considerations regarding disease in old age. *J. Gerontol.* **32**:642 (1977).

Botwinick, J., and Storandt, M. Cardiovascular status, depressive affect, and other factors in reaction time. *J. Gerontol.* **29**:543–548 (1974).

Broadman, K., Erdmann, A. J., Jr., Lorge, I., and Wolf, H. G. The Cornell medical index-health questionnaire. VI. The relation of patient complaints to age, sex, race and education. *J. Gerontol.* **8**:339–342 (1953).

Brunner, H. R., Laragh, J. H., Baer, L., Newton, M. E., Goodwin, F. T., Krakoff, L. R., Bard, R. H., and Buhler, F. R. Essential hypertension: renin and aldosterone, heart attack and stroke. *New Eng. J. Med.* **286**:441–449 (1972).

Desroaches, H. F., Kaiman, B. D., and Ballard, H. T. Factors influencing reporting of physical symptoms by the aged patient. *Geriatrics* **22**:169–175 (1967).

Eisdorfer, C., and Wilkie, F. Stress, disease, aging, and behavior. In J. E. Birren and K. W. Schaie (eds.), *Handbook of the Psychology of Aging*. New York: Van Nostrand Reinhold Co., 1977, pp. 251–275.

Elias, M. F., Elias, P. K., and Elias, J. W. *Basic Processes in Adult Developmental Psychology: An Experimental Approach*. St. Louis: The C. V. Mosby Co., 1977, pp. 221–255.

Enzer, N., Simonson, E., and Blankstein, S. S. Fatigue of patients with circulatory insufficiency, investigated by means of fusion frequency of flicker. *Ann. Internal Med.* **16**:701–707 (1942).

Finch, C. E. Guest editorial. *J. Gerontol.* **32**:257 (1977a).

Finch, C. E. Letters to the editor: response to comments by H. T. Blumenthal. *J. Gerontol.* **32**:642 (1977b).

Friedman, M. J., and Bennet, P. Depression and hypertension. *Psychosomatic Med.* **39**:134–142 (1977).

Goldman, H., Kleinman, K., Snow, M., Bidus, D., and Korol, B. Correlations of diastolic blood pressure and cognitive dysfunction in essential hypertension. *Dis. Nerv. Sys.* **35**:571–572 (1974).

Hertzog, C., Gribbin, K., and Schaie, K. W. The influence of cardiovascular disease and hypertension on intellectual stability. Paper presented at the 28th Annual Meeting Gerontol. Soc., Louisville, Ky., October, 1975.

Hertzog, C., Schaie, K. W., and Gribbin, K. Cardiovascular diseases and changes in intellectual functioning from middle to old age. *J. Gerontol.* **33**:872–833 (1978).

Klisz, D. Neuropsychological evaluation in older persons. In M. Storandt, I. C. Siegler, and M. F. Elias (eds.), *The Clinical Psychology of Aging*. New York: Plenum Press, 1978, pp. 71–95.

Levine, S., Bayat, H. O., and Rehman, R. Letter to the editor. *J. Gerontol.* **32**:358 (1977).

Light, K. C. Slowing of response time in young and middle-aged hypertensive patients. *Exp. Aging Res.* **1**:209–227 (1975).

Light, K. C. Effects of mild cardiovascular and cerebrovascular disorders on serial reaction time performance. *Exp. Aging Res.* **4**:3–22 (1978).

Marx, J. L. Hypertension: a complex disease with complex causes. *Science* **194**:821–825 (1976).

Monroe, R. T., Whiskin, F. E., Bonacich, P., and Jewell, W. O., III. The Cornell medical index questionnaire as a measure of health in older people. *J. Gerontol.* **20**:18–22 (1965).

Obrist, W. D. The electroencephalogram of healthy aged males. In J. E. Birren, R. N. Butler, S. W. Greenhouse, L. Sokoloff, and M. Yarrow (eds.), *Human Aging: A Biological and Behavioral Study*. USPHS Publ. No. 986. Washington, D.C.: U.S. Government Printing Office, 1963.

Obrist, W. D. Cerebral ischemia and the senescent electroencephalogram. In E. Simson and T. H. McGavack (eds.), *Cerebral Ischemia*. Springfield, Ill.: Charles C. Thomas Publisher, 1964.

Obrist, W. D., and Bissell, L. F. The electroencephalogram of aged patients with cardiac and cerebral vascular disease. *J. Gerontol.* **10**:310–315 (1955).

Obrist, W. D., and Busse, E. W. The electroencephalogram in old age. In W. P. Wilson (ed.), *Application of Electroencephalography in Psychiatry: A Symposium*. Durham, N.C.: Duke University Press, 1965.

Obrist, W. D., Busse, E. W., and Henry, C. E. Relation of electroencephalogram to blood pressure in elderly persons. *Neurology* **11**:151–158 (1961).

Pentz, C. A., III, Elias, M. F., Wood, W. G., Schultz, N. R., and Dineen, J. Relationship of age and essential hypertension to neuropsychological test performance. *Exp. Aging Res.* (in press).

Pfeiffer, E. Multidimensional qualitative assessment of three populations of elderly. Paper presented at the 26th Annual Meeting Gerontol. Soc., Miami Beach, Fla., November, 1973.

Reitan, R. M., and Davidson, L. A. *Clinical Neuropsychology: Current Status and Application.* New York: John Wiley & Sons, Inc., 1974.

Schultz, N. R., Dineen, J., Elias, M. F., Pentz, C. A., III, and Wood, W. G. WAIS performance for different age groups of hypertensive and control subjects during administration of a diuretic. *J. Gerontol.* **34**:246–253 (1979).

Siegler, I. C. The terminal drop hypothesis: fact or artifact? *Exp. Aging Res.* **1**:169–185 (1975).

Spieth, W. Cardiovascular health status, age, and psychological performance. *J. Gerontol.* **19**:277–284 (1964).

Spieth, W. Slowness of task performance and cardiovascular disease. In A. T. Welford and J. E. Birren (eds.), *Behavior, Aging, and the Nervous System.* Springfield, Ill.: Charles C. Thomas, Publisher, 1965, pp. 366–399.

Streeten, D. H. P., Schletter, F., Clift, G., Stevenson, C., and Dalakos, T. G. Studies of the renin-angiotensin-aldosterone system in patients with hypertension and normal subjects. *Am. J. Med.* **46**:844–861 (1969).

Szafran, J. Age differences in choice reaction time and cardiovascular status among pilots. *Nature* **200**:904–906 (1963).

Szafran, J. Age differences in sequential decisions and cardiovascular status among pilots. *Aerospace Med.* **36**:303–310 (1965).

Szafran, J. Age, cardiac output and choice reaction time. *Nature* **209**:836 (1966a).

Szafran, J. Age differences in the rate of gain of information signal detection strategy and cardiovascular status among pilots. *Gerontologist* **12**:6–17 (1966b).

Szafran, J. Psychophysiological studies of pilots. In G. A. Talland (ed.), *Human Aging and Behavior.* New York: Academic Press, Inc., 1968.

Thompson, L. W., Eisdorfer, C., and Estes, E. H. Cardiovascular disease and behavior changes in the elderly. In E. Palmore (ed.), *Normal Aging.* Durham, N.C.: Duke University Press, 1970, pp. 227–231.

Thurstone, L. L., and Thurstone, T. G. *Examiner Manual for the SRA Primary Mental Abilities Test.* Chicago: Science Research Associates, Inc., 1949.

Verwoerdt, A. *Clinical Geropsychiatry.* Baltimore: The Williams and Wilkins Co., 1976.

Wilkie, F. L., and Eisdorfer, C. Intelligence and blood pressure in the aged. *Science* **172**:959–962 (1971).

Wilkie, F. L., Eisdorfer, C., and Nowlin, J. B. Memory and blood pressure in the aged. *Exp. Aging Res.* **2**:2–16 (1976).

Wood, W. G., Elias, M. F., Schultz, N. F., and Pentz, C. A., III. Hypertension and symptoms reported on the Cornell medical index. *Exp. Aging Res.* **4**:421–431 (1978).

Wood, W. G., Elias, M. F., Schultz, N. R., and Pentz, C. A., III. Anxiety and depression in young and middle aged hypertensive and normotensive subjects. *Exp. Aging Res.* (in press).

6
A Behavior-Genetic Approach to the Study of Age, Hypertension and Behavior: Testing the Non-Causality Hypothesis *

Merrill F. Elias, Ph.D.

Department of Psychology
University of Maine at Orono
Orono, Maine

INTRODUCTION

In the previous chapter we reviewed a number of studies of the relationship of hypertension, and other vascular diseases, to performance on cognitive tasks. It is clear from this literature that we cannot, for practical, moral, and ethical reasons, exert the kind of control over human studies that would permit definitive answers with regard to direct causal influences of hypertension and other cardiovascular diseases on performance. There are a number of problems with regard to the study of blood pressure–behavior relationships in humans; for example, hypertension cannot be allowed to run its natural course, many important physiological and anatomical studies cannot be done, and extremely large numbers of subjects are required to determine

---

* We wish to thank Dr. Thomas H. Roderick of the Jackson Laboratory, Bar Harbor, Maine, for his critical review of this chapter and his helpful suggestions.

the contribution of genotype to the relationship between vascular disease and performance. For these reasons, animal models for hypertension have great appeal. A comprehensive review of animal studies of hypertension and behavior has been published elsewhere (Elias, 1978).

The purpose of this chapter is to review our studies of hypertension and behavior using mice with high and low blood pressure developed by Gunther Schlager (1974), and, in doing so, to illustrate the potential usefulness of the laboratory mouse as a tool for understanding the relationships among hypertension, aging, and behavior. The review is limited to mice and to hypertension, but it may serve as a model for behavior-genetic research with other species and other diseases.

Early in our studies, several research strategies were considered and then rejected. We considered using invasive procedures which cause sustained elevations in blood pressure and, in some instances, cerebrovascular and cardiovascular pathology; for example, hypothalamic stimulation, interference with sexual and protective reflexes, blasts of air, manipulation of housing, surgery, drugs (see Elias, 1978). However, these manipulations can have an adverse influence on behavior which is difficult to separate from the influence of hypertension per se. Comparison of two or three inbred strains differing with respect to blood pressure values was an equally undesirable strategy (although it has been employed by others), because the observation of behavioral differences among a few strains that differ in blood pressure values does not permit a conclusion that blood pressure extremes per se are related to those behaviors in a causal manner. For example, high blood pressure values and decreased activity level may characterize several strains; low blood pressure values and increased activity level may characterize several others. However, these relationships may exist only by virtue of the fact that these strains differ with respect to many genes and, consequently, with respect to a variety of physiological and behavioral traits which are unrelated, save in the trivial sense that they exist in the same strain.

Our rejection of inbred strain comparisons as a means of studying the relationship of blood pressure extremes to behavior does not indicate that inbred strain comparisons are not useful. They are, as is clear from chapters by Sprott and Goodrick, extremely valuable in a variety of research contexts where genetic control and manipulation are important. In order to relate blood pressure values to behavior it would be necessary to use a battery of strains with minimal common ancestry. This involves large numbers of animals, as multiple strains would have to be assigned to at least three age groups. Even then, additional behavior-genetic manipulations would have to be performed in order to make inferences concerning the genetic basis of any observed relationship between blood pressure values and behavior. Another problem with this approach is that the investigator interested in an animal model for hypertension is interested in the relationship of extreme blood pressure values to behavior, not merely in the relationship of blood pressure per se to behavior. For these reasons we elected to compare two *stocks* of mice genetically *selected* for blood pressure extremes, and then to employ some relatively simple genetic manipulations that allow one to test whether differences in behavior between the high and low blood pressure stocks were causally related to blood pressure extremes.

The basic objective in any selection study is to genetically select (breed) for a behavioral or physiological trait of interest. In the course of selection, *correlated traits* emerge; for example, high brain-weight mice have higher body weights than low brain-weight mice (Roderick, Wimer, and Wimer, 1976). These correlated traits represent "confounding" variables, but they also provide important information about causal relationships between the selected-for trait and the correlated trait. Appropriate genetic and developmental studies with the selected lines can provide important information about the nature of the relationship between brain weight and body weight or high blood pressure and heart weight. This holds true for the relationship between blood pressure and behavior as well; that is, when behavioral differences emerge as a correlate of blood pressure extremes, appropriate genetic manipulations can provide information about the nature of that relationship. In short, the model allows a test of its own usefulness. This point is illustrated by the results of our behavioral studies which are summarized later in this chapter.

A variety of genetically selected hypertensive rat stocks are available. They include the spontaneously hypertensive rat (SHR) and the Dahl hypertensive-sensitive (S) and hypertensive-resistant (R) rat strains (see Elias, 1978). We elected to use Schlager's high and low blood pressure mice (BP I mice) because of our previous work with mice and because they met a number of important criteria for our behavior-genetic investigations: (1) there was a randomly mated control group derived from the same foundation stock as the high and low blood pressure mice, (2) response to selection was very rapid and thus high and low blood pressure lines showed increasing differences in blood pressure values from generation to generation, (3) blood pressure values were greater than those observed for a variety of inbred strains, and (4) a group of F_2 mice (produced by an initial cross of high and low BP I mice) was available for necessary behavior genetic experiments following initial comparisons between high and low lines (stocks). The designation BP I refers to the fact that the mice were produced from Schlager's first selection program for hypertension.

SCHLAGER'S SELECTION PROCEDURE

In order to understand the implications of our behavioral experiments with Schlager's high and low blood pressure (BP I) mice, it is important to review briefly the way in which they were selected. Detailed descriptions may be found in papers by Schlager (1974) and Elias (1978). (Figure 6.1 shows a simplified selection diagram for any selection program.) The BP I mice were developed from a "foundation stock" derived from an eight-way cross of eight inbred strains: LP/J, SJL/J, BALB/cJ, C57BL/6J, 129/J, CBA/J, RF/J, and BDP/J. This was the first eight-way cross by Roderick, Wimer, and Wimer (1976, p. 147). The strains were selected specifically as commonly inbred strains with as little common ancestry as possible. The objective was to maximize genetic variability in the foundation stock. After three generations of random mating of this foundation stock, Schlager began selecting for high and low blood pressure stocks (or lines) by mating male mice with the highest blood pressures to female mice with the highest blood pressures. The same mating strategy was employed for male and female mice with the lowest blood pressures. This procedure (mating mice with extreme blood pressure values) was repeated for successive generations. Some degree of inbreeding does occur in a closed mating system such as this, but the resulting stocks from Schlager's selection program are *not* inbred strains because

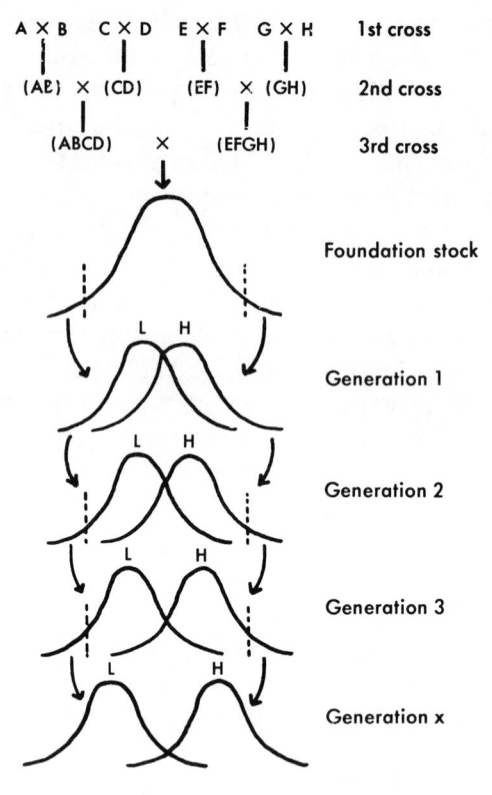

Figure 6.1. A schematic diagram illustrating two-way selection. In this general example, L and H represent extreme values of any phenotype which may be the selected-for trait. Letters at the top of the graph represent inbred strains used to form the foundation stock. In actual practice the distribution of blood pressure values for the high and low lines may not show such rapid separation. Also, animals in the foundation stock are often randomly mated for several generations before selection is begun and a randomly mated control line (or better yet, lines) is (are) maintained for each generation of selection. (From: Elias, Elias, and Elias, 1977. Copyright by The C. V. Mosby Co. Reprinted by permission.)

double first cousin and brother-sister matings were avoided for most of the selection experiment. As an important genetic control, a group of mice from the foundation stock were mated randomly at each generation of selection.

Tail-cuff plethysmography was used to record systolic blood pressure (mm Hg) so that mice with the highest and lowest blood pressures could be selected for mating and so that blood pressures could be recorded for each generation of selection. When appropriate precautions are taken, the "tail-cuff" method has proven to be a reliable index of systolic blood pressure (Bunag, 1971; Pfeffer, Pfeffer, and Frohlick, 1971).

Figure 6.2 shows the results of Schlager's selection experiment for 12 generations. At the 12th generation, means for the high and low blood pressure lines differed by 38 mm Hg for the males and 29 mm Hg for the females. Schlager (unpublished) has reported diastolic blood pressure differences of 40 mm Hg (98 ± 8 mm Hg vs. 59 ± 8 mm Hg) for low and high BP I mice of generation 14, and correlations of $r = 0.94$ ($N = 11$) and $r = 0.97$ ($N = 7$) between direct diastolic recordings from the carotid artery and indirect systolic blood pressure values. A previous review (Elias, 1978) summarizes physiological studies with BP I stocks (p. 130) and discusses the appropriateness of the high and low BP I mice as models for hypertension (pp. 132–139). One of the most important findings was that the high blood pressure mice exhibited higher heart-weight/body-weight ratios than the low blood pressure mice (Florini, Geary, Saito, Manowitz, and Sorrentino, 1975). In this same study, high and low blood pressure stocks differed with respect to several biochemical indexes of cardiac hypertrophy; for example, the high blood pressure mice exhibited a greater rate of protein synthesis in the heart muscle. Table 6.1 compares systolic blood pressure values for the BP I stocks at 12 generations with values for some commonly used inbred strains.

BEHAVIORAL STUDIES WITH THE HIGH AND LOW BP I MICE

Encouraged by (1) the availability of high blood pressure, low blood pressure, and control-line mice from a common foundation stock, (2) the high correlations between diastolic and systolic blood pressure lines reported by Schlager (see Elias, 1978), (3) the large differences in systolic and diastolic blood pressure between the high and low blood pressure lines, and (4) the initial evidence for cardiac hypertrophy in the high blood pressure stocks, we began a behavioral testing program which ultimately resulted in data on the following behavioral variables: time-to-escape from either arm of a two-choice water maze (escape time); time-to-escape from the correct arm of a two-

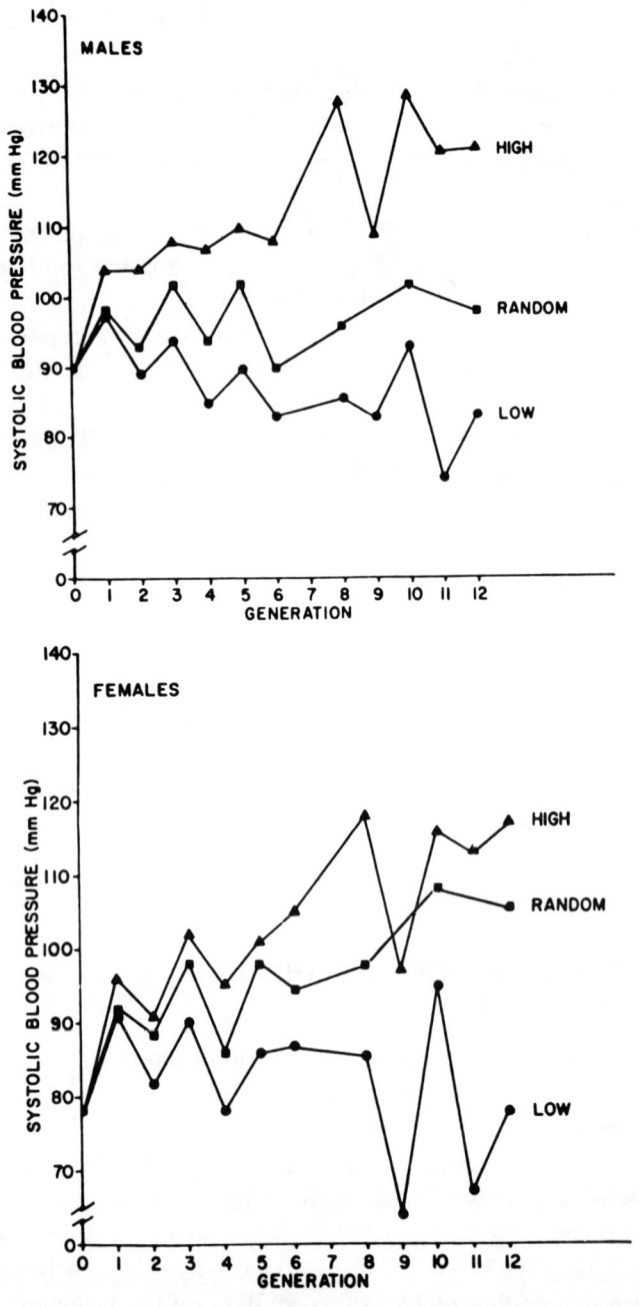

Figure 6.2. A graphic representation of response-to-selection for systolic blood pressure for male (top) and female (bottom) mice. (From: Schlager, 1974. Copyright by *Genetics*. Reprinted by permission.)

Table 6.1. Blood Pressure Values Determined by Schlager for Some Commonly Used Inbred Strains of Mice and for the BP I Mice at 12 Generations of Selection.[a,*]

Strain and Stock	Mean Systolic BP ± SEM from Low to High	N
C3Heb/FeJ	72 ± 1.5	10
A/J	80 ± 1.0	115
BP I (Low female)	85 ± 2.1	43
BP I (Low male)	89 ± 2.0	50
129/J	89 ± 2.0	40
DBA/2J	90 ± 1.5	71
AKR/J	92 ± 4.8	7
C3H/HeJ	93 ± 4.0	15
C57BL/6J	93 ± 2.2	40
A/HeJ	93 ± 3.9	15
RF/J	96 ± 1.8	40
SJL/J	97 ± 1.7	68
CBA/J	97 ± 1.9	40
BALB/cJ	103 ± 1.4	151
SWR/J	110 ± 3.4	18
BP I (High female)	117 ± 2.2	44
BP I (High male)	124 ± 2.7	49

[a] Schlager notes that systolic blood pressures of inbred strains of the same age as the BP I lines are not available, but strains used in the eight-way cross were 8–10 months of age. The differences between the highest (BALB/cJ) and the lowest (BDP/J) of the eight strains was 25 mm Hg and the range was 38 mm Hg; the selected high line was 10 mm higher than any of the inbred strains. All mice from the inbred strains were males.
* Data taken from Schlager, G., and Weibust, R. Genetic control of blood pressure in mice. *Genetics* **55**:497–506 (1967); and Schlager, G. Selection for blood pressure levels in mice. *Genetics* **76**:537–549 (1974). Reprinted with permission from Elias, M. F., Some contributions of genetic selection to the study of hypertension and behavior over the life span: methodologic considerations and useful future directions. In D. Bergsma and D. E. Harrison (eds.), *Genetic Effects on Aging*. Copyright 1978, Alan R. Liss, Inc.

choice water maze (spatial-discrimination escape time); mean trials-to-criterion on original learning, relearning and reversal-learning tasks (water maze–discrimination learning); open-field activity and defecation; corticosterone response-to-stress; mean percent ethanol consumption; and social aggression.

The behavioral battery was *not* selected with the objective of testing specific hypotheses generated from the human literature. Our objective was to compare the high and low blood pressure lines with regard to a variety of laboratory tasks used with mice, and then to perform behavior-genetic manipulations that would enable us to determine whether observed differences between high and low blood pressure stocks represented a causal association between extreme blood pressure values and behavior. However, the choice of several tasks was influenced by the human literature (see Elias, Elias, and Elias, 1977, chapter 12; Elias, 1978) and the previous chapter with respect to studies of cognitive performance, memory, and aggression. One would expect the hypertensive animal to learn less well (particularly reversal-learning problems), to remember less well, and to differ from low blood pressure mice with respect to aggression. The studies of open-field activity, swimming speed, and corticosterone response to a stressor were done primarily to identify behavioral measures that might help to explain differences in learning and memory, and to evaluate the effects of nonlearning factors which influence performance. The studies of alcohol reflected the interests of W. Gibson Wood (Wood, Elias, and Pentz, 1978).

Swimming Escape Time

Elias (1978) has reviewed these studies, and a bibliography of the studies may be found in this paper. In brief, the results were as follows. No consistent differences between blood pressure groups (high vs. low and control) were obtained for mean swimming time to escape from *either* arm of the water maze. Thus, results of our water maze–discrimination learning studies could not be attributed to differences among blood pressure stocks in swimming speed per se.

Discrimination Escape Time

Figure 6.3 summarizes the results of an unpublished study of swimming-discrimination escape times (escape from a water maze). It may be seen that for the older animals, the responses of the high and low blood pressure mice were more divergent for the first several blocks of trials, although both groups exhibited progressive improvement throughout the experiment. No differences between high and low blood pressure mice were observed for the younger mice until the last two blocks of training. A later experiment with a single age group of 17–20-month-old high and low blood pressure mice revealed performance profiles that were almost identical to those observed for the 13–14-month-old mice.

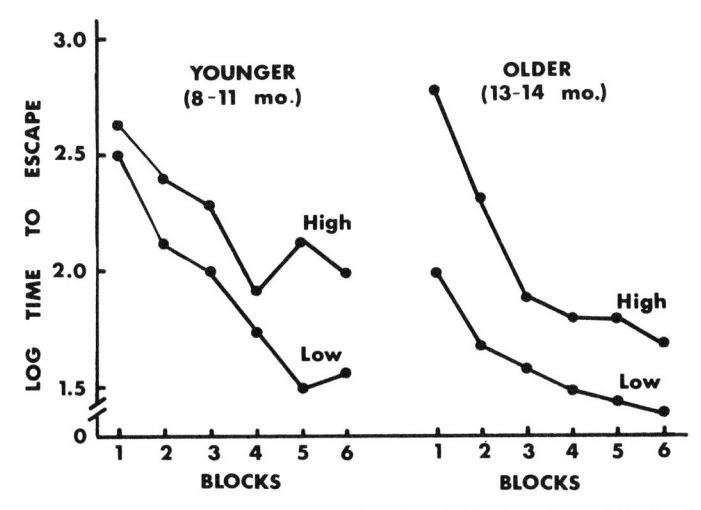

Figure 6.3. Mean time-to-escape (seconds) for 6 blocks of spatial discrimination learning trials for Schlager's high and low blood pressure mice. (From: Elias, 1978. Copyright by Alan R. Liss, Inc. Reprinted by permission.)

Days-to-Criterion

In a study of days-to-criterion performance in the water maze (Elias, Elias, and Schlager, 1973), the high blood pressure mice (BP I) performed less well than the low blood pressure mice (BP I), but there was no age-by-blood pressure interaction and no age main effect. The age groups were the same as those used in the swimming discrimination–escape time study reported above. Failure to find an age effect was related to the fact that the two-choice discrimination tasks were quite simple and very old animals were not tested. However, a more difficult task, discrimination-reversal learning, had to be abandoned because too few of the high blood pressure mice could reach a criterion of 13 correct spatial discriminations in a series of 14 trials.

Open-Field Activity

The open-field data (Elias and Pentz, 1977) is discussed in more detail in a later section. Too few boluses were recorded to permit a meaningful defecation score to be constructed. Low blood pressure mice were more active than high blood pressure mice for three age groups (120 days, 215 days, and 510 days), but not for the oldest age group tested (750 days). The low blood pressure mice exhibited a significant decrease in activity level when comparisons were made between the 510-day-old and the 750-day-old animals.

Alcohol Studies

Results of our percent-ethanol-consumption studies (Wood and Elias, 1978) revealed no age-by-blood pressure interaction, although the high blood pressure mice consumed a higher percentage of ethanol at 6–18% concentrations in comparison to the low blood pressure mice (see Figure 6.4).

Social Aggression Study

Our studies of aggression (Elias, Elias, and Schlager, 1975) were not done with different age groups of animals. Basically, the low blood

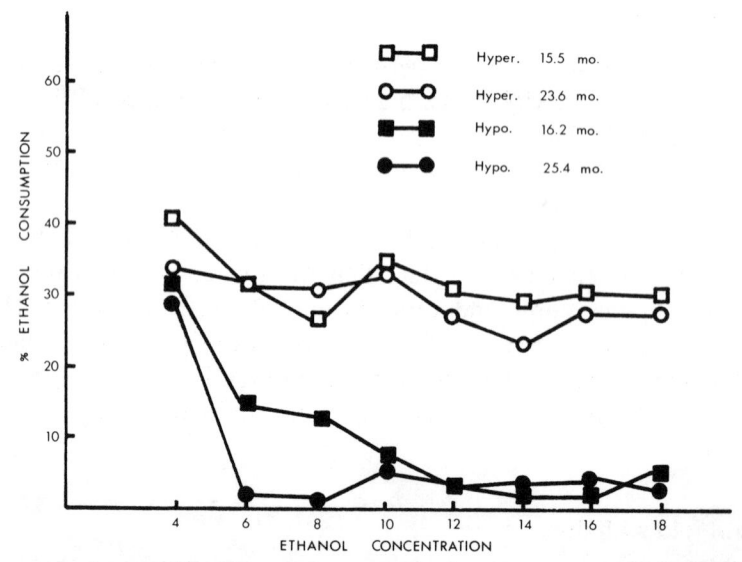

Figure 6.4. Ethanol preference (percent ethanol consumed) at eight ethanol concentrations for the high blood pressure (BP I) and low blood pressure (BP I) mice. *Hyper* refers to high blood pressure and *hypo* refers to low blood pressure. Each point represents the mean for eight animals. (From: Wood, Elias, and Pentz, 1978. Copyright by the *Journal of Studies on Alcohol*. Reprinted by permission.)

pressure mice attacked more than the high blood pressure mice when they were pitted against both high and low blood pressure target mice. More refined analyses of attack behavior indicated that the greatest level of "social aggression" was emitted by the low blood pressure mice when the high blood pressure mice were "targets of attack."

Corticosterone Response-to-Stress

No older animals were tested in the corticosterone study, but the results are of general interest. The high blood pressure mice exhibited greater plasma corticosterone response to open-field stress than did the low blood pressure mice (Pentz, 1976).

TESTS OF CAUSALITY FOR CORRELATED TRAITS

Results of our studies with the "hypertensive mouse" would appear to be rather encouraging with respect to the notion that high blood pressure is associated with inferior water maze learning, decreased activity level, increased ethanol consumption, lower social aggression scores, and, for very young mice, greater corticosterone response-to-stress. One might be tempted to relate the different behavioral findings to each other and to speculate with regard to possible intervening physiological mechanisms. However, speculations regarding relationships between intervening variables and generation of physiological hypotheses are ill-advised in the absence of follow-up tests of the "non-causality hypothesis." Very often these studies are not performed. In some cases the stocks used do not meet criteria necessary for appropriate genetic manipulations. In many cases the investigators are not aware that they can and should be done (see Elias, 1978).

We can best illustrate the testing of "non-causality" by examining our discrimination-learning study in more detail. Table 6.2 shows mean systolic blood pressure values, swim-escape time, original learning (days-to-criterion), relearning (days-to-criterion), and reversal learning (days-to-criterion) for the high and low blood pressure mice from the random control line. As noted previously, the high blood pressure mice required a greater number of trials-to-criterion for both the original learning task and the reversal learning task. There are several possible explanations for these differences in learning per-

Table 6.2. Mean Systolic Blood Pressure Values, Swim-Escape Times, Original Learning, Relearning, and Reversal Learning for the High and Low Blood Pressure Mice that Reached Criterion on Original Learning.*

	BLOOD PRESSURE (MM HG)	(RANGE)	HABITUATION (SECONDS-TO-ESCAPE)	ORIGINAL LEARNING (DAYS-TO-CRITERION)	RELEARNING (DAYS-TO-CRITERION)	REVERSAL LEARNING (DAYS-TO-CRITERION)
H	112	(98–130)	13.2 ± 1.9	43.0 ± 5.5	18.0 ± 2.3	53.0 ± 5.4
R	83	(60–105)	9.8 ± 1.0	28.7 ± 1.6	14.5 ± 1.0	40.7 ± 3.9
L	72	(58–85)	7.1 ± 0.4	26.0 ± 2.7	15.3 ± 0.7	35.3 ± 2.5

NOTE: Two trials were given each day until criterion was met. Criterion = 13/14 correct responses. A greater number of days-to-criterion indicates poorer learning performance. H = high line; R = random line; L = low line.
* From: Elias, M. F. and Schlager, G. S. Discrimination learning in mice genetically selected for high and low blood pressure. *Physiol. Behav.* 13:261–267 (1974); reprinted with permission.

formance: (1) *very direct causal relationship* between blood pressure extremes and performance; for example, hypertension-induced pathology results in performance decrement; (2) *indirect causal relationship* between hypertension and behavior; for example, a set of genes influencing blood pressure also influences behavior (pleiotropy);[1] (3) *non-causal relationship* between blood pressure and behavior; that is, observed relationships reflect a spurious, non-causal association between blood pressure and performance. This "spurious association" explanation does not indicate that extreme blood pressure values cannot have causal effects on performance under any circumstances. Rather it indicates that for high and low blood pressure stocks of mice used, blood pressure and behavioral values are related only in the trivial sense that they happen to co-vary for two different stocks

---

[1] Where one or two genes are associated with the selected-for trait and the correlated trait, a linked-gene phenomenon may also explain the relationship between the two traits; that is, a gene influencing the selected-for trait may be closely linked with a gene influencing the correlated trait. If so, one would expect to see the same results for the original selection lines (high and low BP I lines) and the segregating F_2 generation. Acceptance of the causality hypothesis does not allow the investigator to distinguish between pleiotropic effects or linked-gene effects. The probability of a linked-gene effect is greatly reduced as the number of genes involved in a trait or traits is increased beyond one or two.

(genotypes). Stated empirically, the relationship between blood pressure and performance would not be replicated consistently if the selection experiment were to be repeated over and over.

Fortunately, the hypothesis of spurious association can be tested in a variety of ways. Among others, Roderick, Wimer, and Wimer (1976) have discussed some of the ways in which the nature of relationships among correlated traits can be examined. As noted above, one may repeat the selection experiment and the behavioral tests. Alternatively, one can follow the course of selection generation after generation. If increasing extremes in the selected-for trait (e.g., blood pressure values) are correlated with increasing differences in the behaviors of interest (e.g., trials-to-criterion in the water maze), the investigator may reject the non-causality (spurious association) hypothesis. A far less time-consuming approach is to investigate the relationship between blood pressure and learning performance in a group of genetically heterozygous animals *derived from the same foundation stock* as the selected lines. The randomly mated control line can be used for this purpose or an "F_2 test" can be performed. Table 6.3 summarizes the steps used in the F_2 test, the hypotheses tested, and the implications of accepting or rejecting the non-causality hypothesis.

Table 6.4 summarizes our findings when this test was applied to the trials-to-criterion data. Rather than correlate performance scores and blood pressure for all the F_2 mice, we compared groups with high, moderately low, and low blood pressure. It may be noted that there were no significant differences in days-to-criterion scores even though the blood pressure values for the high blood pressure F_2 mice were similar to those for the high blood pressure BP I mice. These data indicate that the relationship between blood pressure and trials-to-criterion (days-to-criterion) was non-causal. If the relationship between trials-to-criterion scores and blood pressure extremes had been related to genetic pleiotropy (or any other causal mechanism), the high blood pressure groups of the F_2 generation (Table 6.3) would have performed less well than the low blood pressure mice.

The reader is reminded that the rejection of the non-causality hypothesis (acceptance of the causality hypothesis) does not allow the investigator to make inferences as to the *nature* of the causal relationship. It is also important to reinforce the point that the "F_2

Table 6.3. Summary of the Steps Necessary for a Very Simple Test of Non-Causal Relationships Between a Selected Trait (In This Case, Systolic Blood Pressure) and a Correlated Trait (In This Case, Days-to-Criterion in the Water Maze).*

HYPOTHESIS TO BE TESTED	IMPLICATION OF ACCEPTANCE
Null hypothesis: Non-causality	Relationship observed between blood pressure and behavior for the high and low lines reflects an accident of selection.
Alternative hypothesis: Causality	Some causal relationship(s) is (are) involved in the association of days-to-criterion scores and extreme blood pressure values (e.g., pleiotropy; linked genes [a]; very direct causal effect of extreme blood pressure).

STEPS IN TEST

1. Cross high and low blood pressure stocks (lines).
2. Cross resulting F_1 male and female mice.
3. Determine blood pressure values in resulting heterozygous, randomly segregating F_2 stock.
4. Relate blood pressure to behavior of interest (e.g., days-to-criterion):
   a. Correlate blood pressure and behavior for all animals in F_2 generation, or
   b. Compare extreme blood pressure groups within the F_2 generation.[b]

INTERPRETATION OF RESULTS

Low or nonsignificant correlation between blood pressure and behavior,

or   Accept null hypothesis

Nonsignificant differences between extreme blood pressure groups.

Significant correlation of a reasonably high value and in the same direction as relationship between blood pressure and behavior for the high and low lines;

or   Reject null hypothesis [c]

Significant differences between high and low blood pressure groups of the F_2 generation or among several blood pressure groups from the F_2 generation.

---

[a] Where one or more genes are associated with the selected-for trait and the correlated trait, a linked-gene phenomenon may also explain the relationship between the two traits; that is, a gene influencing the selected-for trait may be closely linked with a gene influencing the correlated trait.

[b] If a randomly mated control line from the same foundation stock is maintained for each generation of selection (as they were for Schlager's BP I mice), these same comparisons can be made with those stocks.

[c] Rejection of the null hypothesis allows the investigator to assume that some causal relationship(s) explain the association between the selected-for trait and the correlated trait, but it does not allow the investigator to determine the nature of that relationship. For example, one cannot conclude that pleiotropy rather than linkage explains the relationship.

* From: Elias, M. F. and Schlager, G. S. Discrimination learning in mice genetically selected for high and low blood pressure. *Physiol, Behav.* **13**:261–267 (1974); reprinted with permission.

Table 6.4. Comparisons of Mean Days-to-Criterion Scores for Extreme Blood Pressure Groups from the F_2 Population Produced by an Initial Cross of High and Low Blood Pressure Mice.*

GROUP	N	BLOOD PRESSURE (MM HG SYSTOLIC) MEAN	RANGE	HABITUATION (SECONDS) MEAN ± SEM	ORIGINAL LEARNING (DAYS-TO-CRITERION) MEAN ± SEM
High F_2	18	131	(123–147)	10.6 ± 0.7	36 ± 4.5
Low F_2	22	95	(70–118)	9.7 ± 0.7	32 ± 2.5
Very low F_2	6	78	(70– 85)	9.8 ± 1.4	40 ± 7.4

NOTE: A larger number for days-to-criterion indicates poorer performance. Observe that the very low F_2 group exhibited the poorest performance.
* From: Elias, J. F., and Schlager, G. S. Discrimination learning in mice selected for high and low blood pressure. *Physiol. Behav.* 13:261–267 (1974); reprinted with permission.

test" is only one way in which the non-causality hypothesis can be tested. If a randomly mated control line has been maintained for each generation of selection, the investigator can compare extreme blood pressure groups from this control line or correlate control line blood pressure values with performance scores. In fact, we found no differences between higher and lower blood pressure groups from the control line and a nonsignificant and low correlation between blood pressure values and performance.

In addition to tests of the non-causality hypothesis for mice derived from a common foundation stock, it is often useful to compare high blood pressure mice that have been derived from different foundation stocks. Table 6.5 summarizes an experiment (Elias and Schlager, 1974) that illustrates this kind of comparison. Mice (BP II) with high blood pressure values, but derived from a different foundation stock than the high blood pressure BP I mice, performed just as well in the water maze (trials-to-criterion) as the *low* blood pressure BP I mice. This finding argues against the notion that blood pressure extremes per se cause inferior performance. The F_2 test essentially predicts these results; that is, if blood pressure extremes per se were responsible for inferior learning, one would expect to see inferior learning for extreme blood pressure mice of the F_2 generation as well as for extreme high and low blood pressure mice from the original

Table 6.5. Comparisons Between High and Low Blood Pressure BP I Stocks and High Blood Pressure BP II Stocks.*

GROUP	N	BLOOD PRESSURE (MM HG SYSTOLIC) MEAN	RANGE	HABITUATION (SECONDS) MEAN ± SEM	ORIGINAL LEARNING (DAYS-TO-CRITERION) MEAN ± SEM
High BP I	5	139	(117–154)	9.8 ± 2.5	60 ± 10.3
Low BP I	6	71	(63– 79)	7.9 ± 2.0	25 ± 3.4
High BP II	7	134	(124–138)	6.1 ± 0.9	25 ± 1.0

* From: Elias, J. F., and Schlager, G. S. Discrimination learning in mice genetically selected for high and low blood pressure. *Physiol. Behav.* **13**:261–267 (1974); reprinted with permission.

selection lines. The F_2 test provides additional information with regard to the possibility that pleiotropy or linkage explains the relationship between blood pressure and behavior for the original selection lines. Thus, we perform the F_2 test prior to any other experiments involving different stocks of mice.

An example of the F_2 test of non-causality, within the context of a study on aging, is provided by Figures 6.5 and 6.6. These figures summarize the results of our activity-level studies discussed previously. Figure 6.5 shows the mean systolic blood pressure values for the high and low blood pressure mice at each age, and mean systolic blood pressure values for two extreme blood pressure groups (240 days of age) of the F_2 generation. In all instances, blood pressure differences are statistically significant (figure 6.5). Figure 6.6 shows the results of behavioral testing with these same animals. Note that differences between the 120-, 215-, and 510-day-old animals were statistically significant when high and low blood pressure (BP I) mice were compared, but differences for 240-day-old F_2 high and low blood pressure groups were not significant. Thus, the relationships between blood pressure and activity scores for the original experiment with the high and low blood pressure stocks *cannot* be attributed to a causal relationship between blood pressure and behavior. Speculations about such possible causal mechanisms would have been inappropriate. However, causal relationships between blood pressure and behavior are often implied in animal studies where no tests of

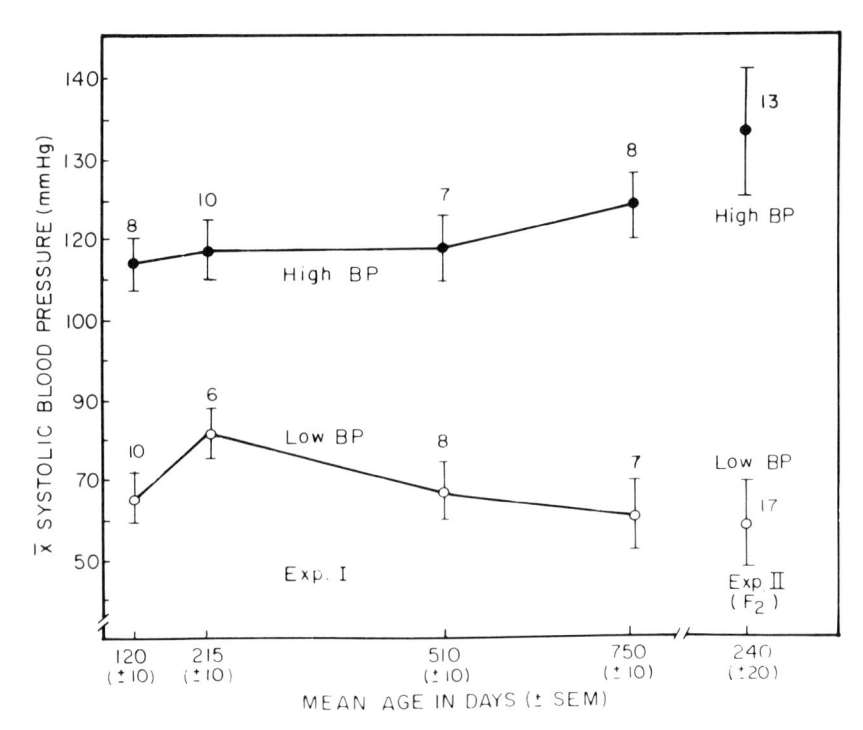

Figure 6.5. Means and standard errors of the mean for blood pressure values (mm Hg) for the high blood pressure (BP I) and low blood pressure (BP I) lines (Exp. I) and for extreme blood pressure groups for the F_2 generation (Exp. II). (From: Elias and Pentz, 1977. Copyright by *Physiology and Behavior*. Reprinted by permission.)

causality have been performed, and in human behavior studies where frequently they are not possible (see Elias, 1978).

One may question whether failures to obtain differences with our F_2 animals were merely failures to replicate chance findings in a statistical sense. This does not seem to provide an adequate explanation. Findings for activity level and trials-to-criterion had been observed in several single-age-group studies before we began our studies on aging (Elias, unpublished).

In addition to the trials-to-criterion data and activity-level data, data for extreme blood pressure groups of the F_2 generation were obtained for aggression scores, water maze discrimination–escape

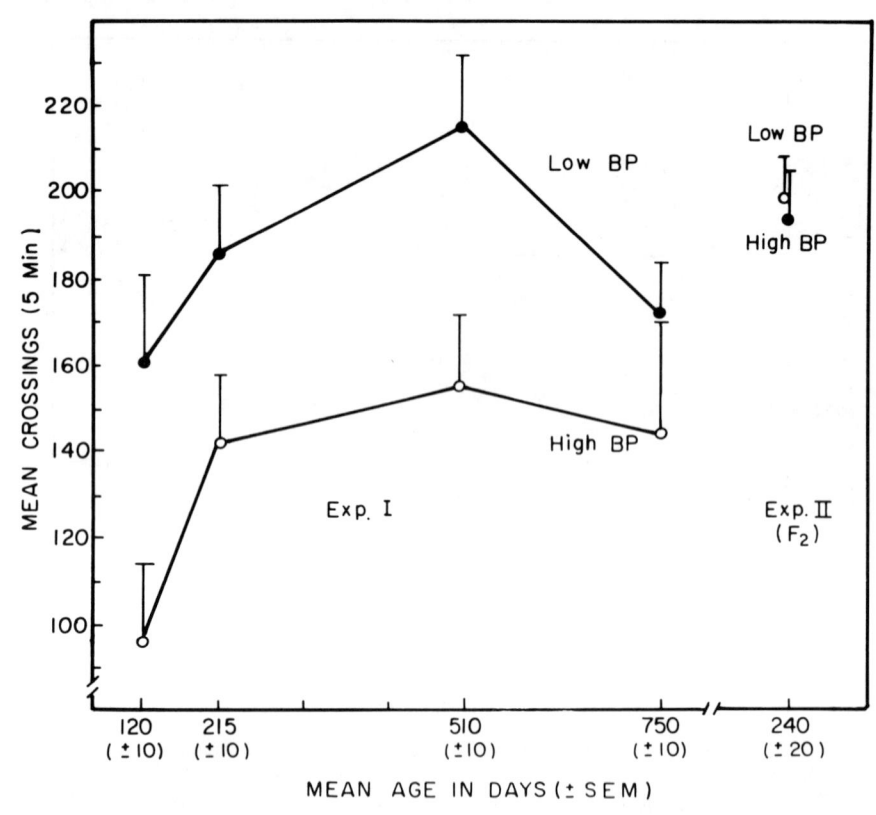

Figure 6.6. Differences in open-field activity levels for high blood pressure (BP I) and low blood pressure (BP I) mice (Exp. I) and for extreme blood pressure groups of the F_2 generation (Exp. II). (From: Elias and Pentz, 1977. Copyright by *Physiology and Behavior*. Reprinted by permission.)

time, and ethanol consumption. Of these five experiments, only the aggression experiment findings were replicated when the F_2 mice were tested. This is not unusual, as the probability is high that a difference in performance between two selected lines does not reflect a causal relationship between the selected-for trait and the correlated trait.

We were disappointed with regard to our repeated failure to reject the non-causality hypothesis. However, it was because we were able to test the validity of the model that we were spared time-consuming and expensive studies designed to determine the causal mechanisms underlying impaired performance in the hypertensive mice.

These data do not indicate that performance decrements observed in hypertensive humans, or even other hypertensive stocks of animals, are unrelated to underlying hypertension-related pathology. They do not indicate that Schlager's mice are of no value in the study of other behaviors or biological traits. They do provide an illustration of the fact that *a relationship between a symptom of disease and behavior does not imply causality, and that there is no substitute for an empirical test of the causality hypothesis, either via genetic manipulations and/or direct investigation of pathological changes.*

PHYSIOLOGICAL STUDIES

Very few physiological studies were performed in our laboratory, as we had a limited number of animals and could not afford to sacrifice them until our behavioral experiments were completed. Given this restraint, it seemed reasonable to employ the following strategy: (1) characterize the relationship between blood pressure and behavior for Schlager's BP I high and low blood pressure stocks; (2) examine blood pressure and behavior relationships for different age groups; (3) determine whether the relationships observed might be accounted for on a basis other than fortuitous accidents of selection; (4) in those instances where the causality hypothesis was accepted, encourage collaborative studies designed to gain further understanding of the physiological and genetic factors contributing to those causal relationships. We were primarily interested in data with respect to learning, performance, ethanol consumption, and activity level in the open-field. Since step 3 indicated that our findings, as a result of steps 1 and 2, were related to an "accident of selection," it was not necessary to invest the time and effort in step 4. It is important to note that physiological traits have no greater immunity to accidental associations with blood pressure phenotype than do behavioral traits. Therefore, the presence of pathology in the central nervous system, had such a finding been observed, would not have precluded the necessity of step 3. A number of physiological studies have been conducted by Schlager and colleagues; see Elias (1978) for a summary and specific references.

FUTURE DIRECTIONS

We have emphasized the fact that behavior-genetic methods can be used to identify behavioral traits which are causally related to blood pressure extremes. We have not exhausted the list of behavioral traits that could be tested with Schlager's mice. However, an important future direction for research on hypertension and behavior with *Mus musculus* is the development of new hypertensive stocks and/or strains. It is important to have additional hypertensive stocks, as Schlager's BP I stocks have some limitations with respect to behavioral experiments. For example, retinal degeneration was present in one of the inbred strains included in the eight-way cross forming the foundation stock from which Schlager's high and low BP I mice were selected, which necessitated the use of spatial discrimination tasks, and the use of dim red illumination for many behavioral tests. One could initiate a new selection program from a second foundation stock (Roderick, Wimer, and Wimer, 1976) free from retinal degeneration. However, neither the new nor the old foundation was developed with selection for hypertensive stocks as an objective. The goal of Roderick's selection program was to obtain a heterogeneous foundation stock from a crossing of inbred strains with minimal common ancestry. Schlager (1974) has pointed out the importance of developing hypertensive stocks from a foundation stock derived from inbred strains exhibiting more extreme blood pressure values than those used to produce the Roderick foundation stock.

A new selection experiment would provide an opportunity to perform behavioral experiments for *successive generations* of selection. This is an excellent way to identify traits that are correlated with blood pressure extremes as a result of pleiotropy or linkage. Pleiotropy or linkage would be indicated if increasing extremes in blood pressure, with successive generations of selection, are accompanied by increasing extremes in correlated behavioral traits.

While efficiency of effort dictates one new selection experiment initially, it would be highly desirable to perform several selection experiments from different foundation stocks. Once new high and low blood pressure stocks are established, brother-sister matings *within* high and low lines could be initiated. The objective here would be to develop a battery of high and low blood pressure strains. Multiple strains allow for increased degrees of freedom when testing causality hypotheses; and since multiple causative factors are responsible for hypertension (Marx, 1976), it is very important to have different models with respect to etiology of hypertension.

Existing batteries of inbred strains, for example, Bailey's recombinant inbred (RI) strains (1971), could be useful in identifying one or a few genes linked to behavior and blood pressure phenotype. However, two factors must be recognized when Bailey's RI strains are employed for research on blood pressure and behavior relationships: (1) they can lead to genetic linkage and identity of genes when phenotypes are influenced by one or a very few genes, and (2) an animal model for hypertension requires extreme blood pressure values. Our studies indicate that blood pressure in Bailey's RI strains is influenced by multiple genes and that the highest and lowest blood pressure values are not as extreme as those observed for Schlager's BP I lines (Elias and Elias, unpublished).

SUMMARY AND CONCLUSIONS

The many problems of control in human studies of behavior, aging, and hypertension have motivated some investigators to turn to animal studies. Animal studies are seductive. They offer control over environmental and genetic variables, the possibility of surgical, pharmacological, and environmental manipulations, and an apparent simplicity of design. However, the development of animal models for the study of hypertension is a time-consuming process that involves more than comparisons among strains of mice that happen to vary with respect to blood pressure. For the most part, animal studies of the relationship between hypertension and behavior (see Elias, 1978) do not go beyond initial strain or stock comparisons. While these studies contribute to the comparative literature, they are no less descriptive than are human studies, despite the fact that better controls are possible. In some instances, the finding of similar relationships between blood pressure and behavior for mice, rats, and humans is offered as evidence for a direct causal association between blood pressure and the behavior in question. However, consistency across species does not provide evidence that those relationships are related to direct causal associations. The "non-causality hypothesis" must be rejected before causal relationships can be assumed. In this chapter, we have provided an example of a simple test of causality that involves rather elementary genetic manipulations.

Results of our "follow-up" behavior-genetic studies with Schlager's high and low blood pressure (BP I) mice have been disappointing because in almost all cases (the exception was aggression), it was necessary to conclude that the observed relationships between blood pressure and behavior were accidental associations. Despite our failure to develop a "behavioral model" for the study of hypertension, we believe that these studies will contribute something of value to the literature if they succeed in calling attention to the fact that erroneous conclusions about causal blood pressure–behavior relationships can result from failure to reject the non-causality hypothesis. The same risks are obviously inherent in any investigations of physiological correlates of behavior.

Our emphasis on *Mus musculus* and on genetic selection by no means implies that these are the only useful tools for the study of disease processes, aging, and behavior with animals. Recombinant inbred strains can provide a very powerful genetic tool in those instances where a behavioral or physiological phenotype is related to one or two major genes (see Bailey, 1971; or Elias, Elias, and Elias, 1977, for a summary for the non-geneticist). Similarly, single-gene mutations in mice have considerable potential as models for the study of a variety of disease processes, including neurological diseases and diabetes (see Russell and Sprott, 1975).

There has been a growing interest in the relationships among hypertension, behavior, and aging in recent years. Because of the attention this problem has received, many investigators in the area of aging seem to assume that hypertension causes inferior performance. They include essential hypertension among the factors that contribute an age bias in the direction of poorer performance for older persons. They tend to at least partially accept the notion that hypertensive individuals perform less well than normotensive individuals because of alterations in cerebral blood flow or lesions of the cerebral vasculature. Presently, we do not have enough data to substantiate these generalizations. While there is ample evidence for pathological changes associated with standard hypertension, we do not yet have data which confirms the hypothesis that specific hypertension-related pathologies cause cognitive deficit. Relevant data will not be forthcoming from animal studies if investigators fail to go beyond the same kinds of descriptive studies with animals that can be done with humans. Taking advantage of possibilities for genetic control and genetic manipulations of animal stocks is a very important step in the right direction. These kinds of studies involve a very large investment of money, time, and physical resources. Great numbers of animals are necessary when behavior-genetic and aging studies are combined. We are not particularly optimistic with regard to federal or institutional support for animal studies dealing with the *behavior*-genetics of hypertension in aging mice or rats. It has been our experience that the demand for relevance in behavioral research is often translated as a need for more descriptive research with human subjects rather than adequate research with animals on a problem of critical relevance to man.

REFERENCES

Bailey, D. W. Recombinant inbred strains. An aid to finding identity, linkage, and function of histocompatibility and other genes. *Transplantation* 11:325–327 (1971).

Bunag, R. D. Pressor effects of the tail-cuff method in awake normotensive and hypertensive rats. *J. Lab. Clin. Med.* 78:675–682 (1971).

Elias, J. W., Elias, M. F., and Schlager, G. Aggressive social interaction in mice genetically selected for blood pressure extremes. *Behav. Biol.* 13:155–166 (1975).

Elias, M. F. Some contributions of genetic selection to the study of hypertension and behavior over the life span: methodologic considerations and useful future directions. In D. Bergsma and D. E. Harrison (eds.), *Genetic Effects on Aging*. National Foundation: March of Dimes, Birth Defects Original Article Series. Vol. XIV. New York: Alan R. Liss, Inc., 1978, 121–156.

Elias, M. F., Elias, J. W., and Schlager, G. Difference in learning for mice selectively bred for high and low blood pressure. Paper presented at the 81st Ann. Conven. Amer. Psychol. Assoc., Montreal, Canada, August 1973.

Elias, M. F., and Elias, P. K. Systolic blood pressure values for Bailey's recombinant inbred strains (Unpublished).

Elias, M. F., Elias, P. K., and Elias, J. W. *Basic Processes in Adult Developmental Psychology*. St. Louis: The C. V. Mosby Co., 1977, pp. 221–255.

Elias, M. F., and Pentz, C. A., III. Blood pressure extremes and activity in aging mice. *Physiol. Behav.* 19:811–813 (1977).

Elias, M. F., and Schlager, G. Discrimination learning in mice genetically selected for high and low blood pressure. *Physiol. Behav.* 13:261–267 (1974).

Florini, J. R., Geary, S., Saito, Y., Manowitz, E. J., and Sorrentino, R. N.

Changes in protein synthesis in heart. In V. J. Cristofalo, J. Roberts, and R. C. Adelman (eds.), *Exploration in Aging.* New York: Plenum Press, 1975, pp. 149–162.

Marx, J. L. Hypertension: a complex disease with complex causes. *Science* **194**:821–825 (1976).

Pentz, C. A., III. The effects of the maternal environment on the behavior of mice genetically selected for low and high blood pressure. Thesis submitted for the degree of Master of Arts in Psychology, Syracuse, New York, April 1976.

Pfeffer, J. M., Pfeffer, M. A., and Frohlick, E. D. Validity of an indirect tail-cuff method for determining systolic arterial pressure in unanesthetized normotensive and spontaneously hypertensive rats. *J. Lab. Clin. Med.* **78**:957–962 (1971).

Roderick, T. H., Wimer, R. E., and Wimer, C. C. Genetic manipulation of neuroanatomical traits. In L. Petrinovich and J. L. McGaugh (eds.), *Knowing, Thinking and Believing: A Festschrift for Professor David Krech.* New York: Plenum Press, 1976, pp. 143–178.

Russell, E. S., and Sprott, R. L. Genetics and the aging nervous system. In G. J. Maletta (ed.), *Survey Report on the Aging Nervous System.* USPHS Publ. No. 74–296. Washington, D.C.: U.S. Government Printing Office, 1974.

Schlager, G. Selection for blood pressure levels in mice. *Genetics* **76**:537–549 (1974).

Wood, W. G., Elias, M. F., and Pentz, C. A. Ethanol preference in genetically selected hypertensive and hypotensive mice. *J. Stud. Alcohol* **39**:820–827 (1978).

7
Age Differences and Age Changes in Cognitive Performance: New "Old" Perspectives

David Arenberg

National Institute on Aging
Gerontology Research Center
Baltimore City Hospital
Baltimore, Maryland

Elizabeth A. Robertson-Tchabo

Department of Human Development
University of Maryland
College Park, Maryland

INTRODUCTION

The purpose of this chapter is to present the experimental research evidence that indicates diminished performance on learning, memory, and problem-solving tasks late in life, and to discuss some ramifications of these findings. There is a pervasive belief (and fervent hope) among gerontologists that intellectual functioning does not decline, even late in life, except shortly before death. It is a very appealing notion and it is obvious why it has been accepted so readily. This view has been based primarily on longitudinal psychometric data that have been collected by Professor Warner Schaie and his colleagues (Schaie and Strother, 1968a and b; Schaie and Labouvie-Vief, 1974; Schaie, Labouvie, and Buech, 1973). Although Baltes and Schaie (1976; Schaie and Baltes, 1977) stated explicitly that they have never claimed that all intellectual abilities are maintained to late life, their use of the phrase "the myth of intellectual decline" (Baltes and Schaie, 1974) has reinforced this view. Recently in response to a critical paper (Horn and Donaldson, 1976), Baltes and Schaie (1976) clarified their use of the term "myth," which they defined as "an uncritically accepted belief." Unfortunately, many readers interpreted "myth" to mean "contrary to fact" or "imaginary." As a result, many elderly individuals and many persons providing services to the elderly now believe that intellectual functioning is maintained even late in life.

In this chapter, intellectual functioning will be defined more broadly than performance on standardized psychometric tests of intelligence, and will include cognitive functioning. Cognition refers to the processes by which sensory input is transformed, reduced, elaborated, stored, and retrieved. Like many terms in everyday use, cognitive functioning causes no problems in common usage, but ceases to be straightforward when subjected to critical inspection. The study of aging and cognitive functioning has followed several independent traditions in the psychology of cognition. One way in which cognitive functioning has been investigated has been concerned almost exclusively with the acquisition and retention of verbal information using rote paired-associate or serial learning tasks, or free recall. The tradition has been to separate the study of verbal memory from the study of nonverbal activities and psychomotor skills.

A further complicating factor in the study of learning and memory is that the processes involved are extremely complex. New information must be registered, stored, and retrieved on demand. Any observed decline in performance with increasing age could be due to a failure in any or all of these processes, and many experimental psychologists would subdivide these stages of processing even further.

This chapter consists essentially of two parts. The first part is a selected review of the literature concerning age and cognitive functioning, including studies based on self-reported memory impairment, on psychometric longitudinal data, and on experimental longitudinal measures.

The second part addresses issues related to the practical concerns of cognitive competence. We will contrast, briefly, abilities and information-processing views of intellectual functioning. We will then consider the relative importance of age differences and age changes as predictors of cognitive competence. Finally, we will discuss possible intervention strategies to improve the level of cognitive performance of some elderly individuals. The second part is necessarily speculative compared to the first part of the paper, but this reflects the knowledge gap in the gerontological literature between description and remediation of cognitive performance.

SELECTED FINDINGS

Self-Report Studies

In addition to the lay view that memory impairment is an intrinsic characteristic of the aging process, some studies have reported subjective, self-report data concerning the prevalence of memory complaints in the elderly. For example, Lowenthal, Berkman, and associates (1967) studied 600 noninstitutionalized residents of San Francisco and found that by age 75, about 66% of the sample were expressing concern about their memory loss. However, frequency of memory complaints does not necessarily correlate with performance on objective tests of memory (Perlin and Butler, 1963; Kahn, Zarit, Hilbert, and Niederhe, 1975).

Kahn and co-workers (1975) studied the relationship between memory complaint and cognitive performance in normal, depressed, and brain-damaged groups of elderly subjects. They found an incongruence between memory complaint and memory performance. Persons without depression and with normal brain function, measured by the Mental Status Questionnaire and the Face-Hand Test (Kahn, Goldfarb, Pollack, and Peck, 1960), performed better on memory tests than brain-damaged individuals. Nondepressed, brain-damaged individuals had a low degree of complaint and poor memory performance, whereas depressed subjects had good memory performance, but high levels of memory complaint. Nevertheless, the fact that an older individual's objective memory performance is similar to the performance of his age peers does not necessarily invalidate his memory complaint. The self-perception that performance has declined from a previously higher level may be accurate. Kahn and his associates appear to imply an antecedent-consequent relationship, that depression results in memory complaint. However, the alternative position—that perceived memory dysfunction leads to depression—seems equally viable in the absence of longitudinal data. Moreover, some individuals may be depressed and have organic brain damage.

Longitudinal Studies

Studies of aging and cognitive functioning consist almost entirely of cross-sectional research designs. In such investigations, two or more adult age groups of different individuals, born at different times, are compared on some measure of cognitive performance. A longitudinal design measures changes in performance in the same individual with increasing age. The cross-sectional approach provides measures of age differences, whereas the longitudinal approach provides measures of changes with age. At best, cross-sectional results approximate changes with age; at worst, they can be extremely misleading. Comparisons of independent samples from the same birth cohort measured at different times, a variant of the longitudinal approach, provide estimates of mean changes, but not of individual changes.

Reports of longitudinal studies vary with respect to findings. One reason for the discrepancy may be differences in the nature of the tasks. Longitudinal studies of intellectual functioning, as measured by intelligence tests, have emphasized little or no decline in abilities with increasing age except shortly before death (e.g., Baltes and Schaie, 1974). Longitudinal studies of cognitive processes, such as learning and memory, have shown consistently that there are age changes late in life (Arenberg, 1978, in press; Arenberg and Robertson-Tchabo, 1977; Gilbert, 1973).

Interpretations of findings also vary. Botwinick (1977), after reviewing the available literature on psychometric intelligence tests, concluded that a decline in intellectual ability is clearly an integral part of the aging process. Evidence for a decrement in performance late in life can be found even in data that were interpreted as showing little or no decline. Age gradients for five selected subtests of the Primary Mental Abilities Test were reported in two studies (Schaie and Strother, 1968a and b). The selected subtests were Verbal Meaning, Number, Space, Word Fluency, and Reasoning. The test-retest interval was 7 years. In both studies, the mean performance declined in all five subtests for the cohorts which had been 60 years and over when measured initially. Similarly, Schaie, Labouvie, and Buech (1973) compared three independent samples of the same birth cohort measured at different times; and Schaie and Labouvie-Vief (1974) described analyses of repeated measures of three-point data covering a 14-year period. Again, for the cohorts age 60 years and over when measured initially, the mean performance declined for each of the five subtests in both types of comparisons. The average declines over 7 years and even over 14 years were not large, but the consistency of the declines indicated that there were age changes in intellectual performance as measured by psychometric intelligence tests.

Evidence for age changes in several aspects of cognitive performance, particularly late in life, can be found in reports from the Baltimore Longitudinal Study (Arenberg, 1974, 1978, in press). Prior to 1978, the participants in the Baltimore Longitudinal Study of Aging (BLSA) were men, predominantly white, educated, and of high socioeconomic status; since 1978, women have been added to the study. The participants visit the Gerontology Research Center of the National Institute on Aging for at least 2.5 days every 2 years. Many physiological, biochemical, medical, and psychological measures and indexes are included in the study.

Performance on the Benton Visual Retention Test (Benton, 1963) has been analyzed more extensively than any of the other cognitive tasks in the BLSA. In this test, each of ten designs, consisting of geometric figures, is presented for 10 seconds, and the task is to reproduce the design from memory, self-paced. Magnitude of change was related to age in the analyses of repeated measures 6 years apart. Mean changes were small or nil for the men initially in their thirties and forties, modest for the men initially in their fifties and sixties, but substantial for the men initially 70 or older. Similar results were found in a replication (see Table 7.1). The changes with age were similar to the cross-sectional age differences (Arenberg, 1978). Recent regression

Table 7.1. Mean Errors for First and Second Measures of the Benton Visual Retention Test for Two Longitudinal Samples.*

INITIAL AGE	N	FIRST MEASURES 1960–1964 [a] 1ST $\bar{X}$	2ND $\bar{X}$	CHANGE $\bar{X}$	N	FIRST MEASURES 1965–1968 [b] 1ST $\bar{X}$	2ND $\bar{X}$	CHANGE $\bar{X}$
30's	48	2.65	3.00	0.35				
40's	70	2.70	2.99	0.29	26	3.08	3.00	−0.08
50's	77	3.36	3.97	0.61	22	4.32	4.64	0.32
60's	45	4.93	5.53	0.60	17	4.94	5.59	0.65
70's	24	6.33	9.33	3.00	8	5.50	8.75	3.25

[a] Mean interval between measures = 6.7 years.
[b] Mean interval between measures = 6.5 years.
* Adapted from Arenberg, D. Differences and changes with age in the Benton Visual Retention Test. *J. Gerontol.* 33:534–540 (1978).

analyses of first-time measures comparable to Schaie's sequential analyses of independent samples confirmed the repeated-measures results. Estimates of magnitude of age decline in performance; that is, within-birth-cohort slopes of errors regressed on calendar time (see Figure 7.1), were highly correlated with age (Arenberg, 1979).

Substantial changes with age in mean performance were also found late in life on two tasks of verbal learning in the BLSA (Arenberg, in press; Arenberg and Robertson-Tchabo, 1977). In paired-associate learning, which required learning to respond with a specific word to each of eight sets of (two) consonants, the pattern of mean changes in performance at the fast pace was similar to the longitudinal Benton results. The youngest men improved slightly 6 years later, the next two older groups (mean ages initially 41.4 and 50.0) declined somewhat, the next two older groups (mean ages initially 57.5 and 66.7) declined substantially, and the oldest group declined dramatically (see Table 7.2). At the slower pace, when more time was provided to respond, all age groups declined in mean performance, and the two oldest groups declined the most (see Table 7.3).

In serial learning, the other verbal learning task, twelve words were presented in sequence, and the sequence was repeated until the list was learned; that is, the next word was responded without error for each word in the list. At the fast pace, the youngest groups improved, but the two oldest groups declined somewhat in mean performance

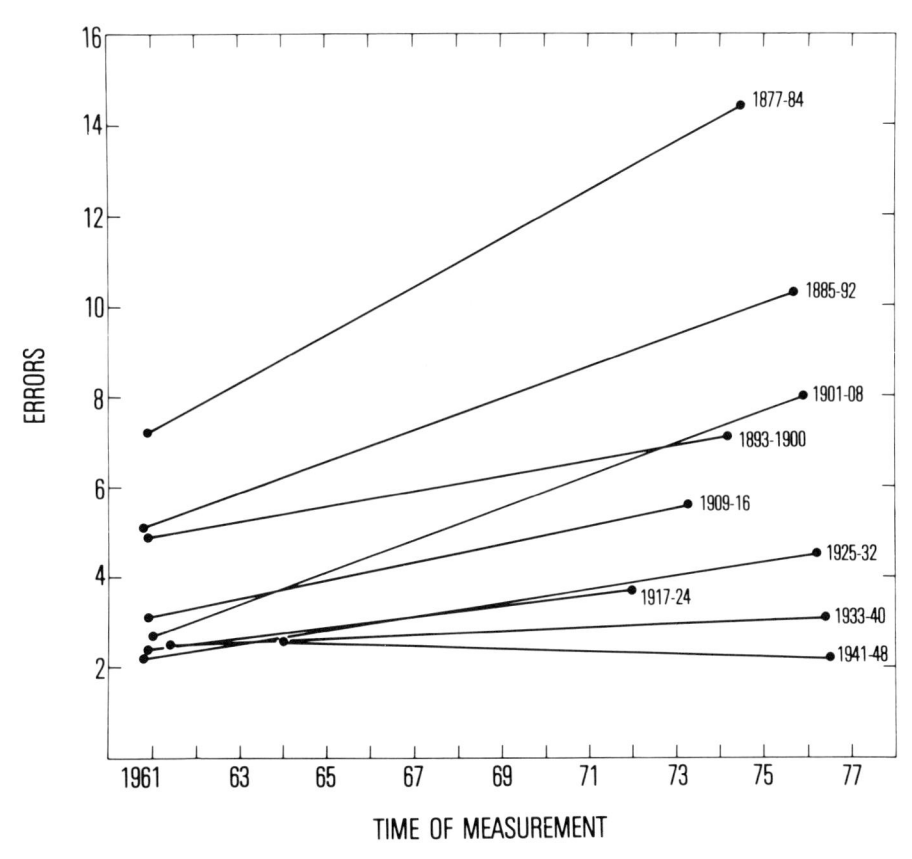

Age Differences and Age Changes in Cognitive Performance 145

Figure 7.1. First-time performance (total errors) on Benton Visual Retention Test regressed against calendar time (1960–1976) for nine birth cohorts from the Baltimore Longitudinal Study of Aging (rho = 0.92 between magnitude of slope, i.e., estimate of age change within cohort, and mean age of cohort).

(see Table 7.4). At the slower pace, mean changes were small for the youngest groups with some improving and others declining, but the oldest group declined precipitously (see Table 7.5).

In a study of logical problem solving in the BLSA, complex problems required reasoning the sequence of switches which would illuminate the goal light. For each problem, the pairs of lights which were related and the direction of each relationship was indicated, but the specific relationship (of three possibilities) was not provided. Ideally,

Table 7.2. Mean Errors for First and Second Measures of Paired-Associate Learning: Short Anticipation Interval.*

INITIAL AGE $\bar{X}$	N	1ST $\bar{X}$	2ND $\bar{X}$	CHANGE $\bar{X}$
34.4	15	68.5	60.9	−7.6
41.4	27	65.6	83.9	18.3
50.0	25	61.6	82.9	21.3
57.5	16	89.1	140.4	51.3
66.7	11	130.4	167.0	36.6
71.4	8	162.8	240.3	77.5

NOTE: Mean interval between measures = 6.8 years.
* Adapted from Arenberg, D., and Robertson-Tchabo, E. A. Learning and aging. In J. E. Birren and K. W. Schaie (eds.), *Handbook of the Psychology of Aging*. New York: Van Nostrand Reinhold Co., 1977, p. 423.

the problem solver would identify the relationships and use that information to determine the solution sequence. The proportions of men who solved the problems decreased with age at the first time of measurement and also 6 years later, but the proportions did not change. For those men who solved the problem both times, measures of effectiveness in reasoning could be obtained and compared longitudinally. A mean decline in effectiveness in reasoning was found only for the group over 70 when measured initially (see Table 7.6). It

Table 7.3. Mean Errors for First and Second Measures of Paired-Associate Learning: Long Anticipation Interval.*

INITIAL AGE $\bar{X}$	N	1ST $\bar{X}$	2ND $\bar{X}$	CHANGE $\bar{X}$
35.5	13	57.9	72.5	14.6
41.5	24	38.6	64.6	26.0
50.9	32	49.8	71.6	21.8
57.5	15	67.4	95.2	27.8
65.4	17	79.1	123.8	44.7
72.1	10	84.2	124.0	39.8

NOTE: Mean interval between measures = 6.7 years.
* Adapted from Arenberg, D., and Robertson-Tchabo, E. A. Learning and aging. In J. E. Birren and K. W. Schaie (eds.), *Handbook of the Psychology of Aging*. New York: Van Nostrand Reinhold Co., 1977, p. 423.

Table 7.4. Mean Errors for First and Second Measures of Serial Learning: Short Anticipation Interval.*

INITIAL AGE $\bar{X}$	N	1ST $\bar{X}$	2ND $\bar{X}$	CHANGE $\bar{X}$
34.4	13	94.9	72.2	−22.7
41.5	28	109.5	89.8	−19.7
50.1	26	107.3	87.3	−20.0
57.9	16	111.1	88.3	−22.8
66.5	13	160.5	171.4	10.9
72.3	8	230.3	234.5	4.2

NOTE: Mean interval between measures = 6.7 years.
* Adapted from Arenberg, D., and Robertson-Tchabo, E. A. Learning and aging. In J. E. Birren and K. W. Schaie (eds.), *Handbook of the Psychology of Aging*. New York: Van Nostrand Reinhold Co., 1977, p. 424.

should be noted that in order to be included in the repeated-measures analyses of reasoning effectiveness, it was necessary for the problem to be solved correctly at both times of measurement. As a result, only the best problem solvers in the oldest groups could be included.

In summary, the longitudinal studies of cognitive performance from the BLSA showed declines with age over an interval of 6 years, particularly late in life. These declines were found for measures of memory, verbal learning, and problem solving. Typically, magnitude of

Table 7.5. Mean Errors for First and Second Measures of Serial Learning: Long Anticipation Interval.*

INITIAL AGE $\bar{X}$	N	1ST $\bar{X}$	2ND $\bar{X}$	CHANGE $\bar{X}$
35.4	14	55.5	63.6	8.1
41.6	26	62.5	48.2	−14.3
51.0	27	53.2	55.3	2.1
57.5	13	89.1	80.8	− 8.3
65.8	15	99.7	106.3	6.6
72.5	7	81.4	187.0	105.6

NOTE: Mean interval between measures = 6.7 years.
* Adapted from Arenberg, D., and Robertson-Tchabo, E. A. Learning and aging. In J. E. Birren and K. W. Schaie (eds.), *Handbook of the Psychology of Aging*. New York: Van Nostrand Reinhold Co., 1977, p. 424.

Table 7.6. Mean Number of Uninformative "Questions" in a Logical Problem: Repeated Measures.*

INITIAL AGE $\bar{X}$	N	1ST $\bar{X}$	2ND $\bar{X}$	CHANGE $\bar{X}$
<40	32	5.28	4.00	−1.28
40's	62	6.71	3.90	−2.81
50's	59	7.07	5.39	−1.68
60's	24	6.96	5.08	−1.88
>70	16	6.62	11.37	4.75

NOTE: Mean interval between measures = 6.7 years.
* Adapted from Arenberg, D. A longitudinal study of problem solving in adults. *J. Gerontol.* **29**:650–658 (1974).

change with age was related to age. The oldest men not only performed more poorly initially, but they also had the largest declines.

It should be noted that these declines with age in cognitive performance were found for an elite group of men. They were not only considerably more highly educated and more economically secure than the general population, but they were healthier as well. Furthermore, the men who returned for second measures 6 years after the first were a select subsample of the men who entered the study. With these positive biases operating, the changes with age that were found probably underestimate the magnitudes of change in the general population. It will be interesting to see whether the results from the Baltimore Longitudinal Study of women will parallel those for the men, particularly with respect to the age at which one begins to find a significant age change, given the significantly longer average life expectancy of women.

The conclusion that there are age changes in several aspects of cognitive performance is based on group mean performance. In every age group, including the oldest, there were some individuals whose level of performance did not decline. Some older individuals' performances are indistinguishable from those of young adults. A systematic investigation of such individual differences and their relationship to level and change of other important variables, such as personality traits (Robertson-Tchabo, Arenberg, and Costa, 1979) or cardiovascular health status (Hertzog, Schaie, and Gribbin, 1978), may help to explain why some people decline and others do not.

AGE DIFFERENCES AND AGE CHANGES AS PREDICTORS OF COGNITIVE COMPETENCE

Although there are statistically significant declines in cognitive functioning late in life, we do not know the practical significance of changes in measures; for example, a small increase in the number of errors on the Benton test. Clearly, an important research goal at this time is to establish the concurrent and predictive validity of the experimental measures. We may speculate that an older individual who perceives increased difficulty in the acquisition of new information may be less likely to take advantage of free adult education programs, or that an individual who observes a decrease in his speed of response might avoid driving in heavy traffic. Similarly if an individual accepts such changes as part of "normal aging," he may not consider remedial steps, and even if intervention techniques were available, he might decline therapy because of a belief that such changes are not only inevitable, but immutable.

Furthermore, it is necessary to maintain a perspective on the implications of age-change and age-difference findings with respect to questions of practical concern. In much that has been written about longitudinal cognitive findings, the question of age change has been confused with the question of competence. Longitudinal studies, and their variants, are necessary to address the question of age changes, but it is not necessary to measure or to estimate age changes to assess current competence. Competence is defined by a level of performance. (Of course, consideration of previous level could be important in choosing a particular intervention strategy.) In practical settings, it is the level of performance, rather than a change in performance, that correlates with competence in activities of daily living (see Cyr and Stone, 1977). For example, an immediate memory span of four items may be essential for compliance with a drug regimen. One individual may have changed three units dropping from an initial span of eight items to five items, whereas a second individual may have changed only one unit from four to three. Despite the fact that the first individual had changed more, it is likely, if other noncognitive factors were equivalent, that he would be more successful than the second person in taking the medication as prescribed.

PSYCHOMETRIC VERSUS INFORMATION-PROCESSING APPROACHES TO COGNITION

Rehabilitation may be viewed as an educational process requiring the acquisition of new information and skills. The need for rehabilitation is determined by a disability, that is, by an unacceptable or insufficient *level* of performance. The most direct approach to remediation is to study a specific behavior and to investigate conditions which affect the level of performance. The purpose of the research would be to identify those aspects of the task that influence or compromise aspects of competent performance.

Before considering strategies for cognitive skill training for some elderly individuals, we will briefly discuss two general approaches to the study of cognitive functioning.

A psychological test may be defined as an objective and standardized measure of a sample of behavior (Anastasi, 1976). The predictive value of a psychometric test depends on the degree to which it serves as an indicator of a relatively broad and significant area of behavior. It should be noted that test items need not resemble closely the behavior which the test is to predict, since the criterion of test evaluation is the extent to which there is an empirically demonstrated relationship between a subject's performance on that test and in other situations. The focus of psychometric theories of intelligence is at a molar abilities level.

Information-processing views of cognitive functioning place emphasis on the acquisition, storage, and utilization of information (see Kintsch, 1970; Melton and Martin, 1972; Neisser, 1967).

Information-processing models view the sequences of operations and transformations involved in cognitive activity between stimulus input and performance output as a complex system with many interacting stages. By examining the relationship between the contents of the input and the contents of the output, measured at various times after presentation of the information, hypotheses are formulated concerning the properties of the flow of information in the nervous system. A basic assumption is that the output is not an immediate consequence of stimulation, but rather is the product of a number of decision processes at successive levels of recoding. In other words, an investigator adopting an information-processing model takes a basic view of man as an active processor of experience (Mahoney, 1974).

In many experimental information-processing models, a distinction is made between two major dimensions of cognitive processing: structural features and control processes (Atkinson and Shiffrin, 1968). Structure refers to permanent features of the system, including both the physical system and the built-in processes that are fixed from one situation to another. Control processes, on the other hand, refer to features that can be readily modified or reprogrammed by an individual and may vary substantially from one time to another, depending upon such factors as the nature of instructions, the meaningfulness of the information, and an individual's experience. The significance of this distinction for aging research is that it is important to isolate the age-related components of performance which an individual can control from the structural, limiting features of the system. The task for the geropsychologist is to optimize a person's use of control processes within the given structural limitations.

It is not our intention to advocate the use of a psychometric or an information-processing view of cognitive functioning, but rather to suggest that both approaches have limitations. Each view may contribute different and important information to the design of individualized cognitive skill training programs for some elderly individuals.

One difference between the psychometric and experimental approaches to cognitive functioning is that the former tends to be subject-oriented whereas the latter is more task-oriented. Eysenck (1977, p. 274) stated: "As a generalization, researchers interested in cognition and information processing have ignored individual differences whereas those concerned with individual differences in intelligence have typically been uninterested in theoretical conceptualizations of the processes involved in intelligent behavior." A psychometric approach to rehabilitation, with its focus on individual differences, can identify abilities that correlate with incompetence or even predict incompetence; that is, individuals at risk may be identified. Although experimental psychologists interested in aging and cognitive functioning have tended to ignore individual differences in intelligence, personality traits, and health status, there is increasing recognition that such variables must be considered systematically as gerontologists accept the challenge to develop cognitive skill training for elderly individuals.

A second difference between the psychometric and information-processing views of cognitive functioning is that, in contrast to the molar focus of psychometric theories of intelligence, information-processing theorists tend to focus on relatively molecular aspects of task performance, such as attention, encoding, storage, and retrieval. Cattell (1971, p. 42) recognized that, "Not nearly enough steps and aspects of the learning and recall process . . . such as immediate committing to memory, rate of fading, mode of retrieval, and other manifestations important to the memorizing processes . . . have been used by psychometrists, who have tended instead to confine themselves to some total learning effect."

However, neither identification of abilities related to level of performance nor identification of components of information processing translate directly to ways to modify cognitive performance The most direct approach to remediation for an individual would appear to be a functional analysis of performance (see Meichenbaum, 1977) on a specific task that requires remediation.

MODIFIABILITY OF COGNITIVE PERFORMANCE

A position that there are significant changes in cognitive performance late in life does not preclude the possibility of changing the levels of performance, either by restructuring the task or environmental conditions, or by specific cognitive skill training. On the contrary, such a position accentuates the need for the development of intervention strategies, particularly for the 10% of the elderly population (Kay, Beamish, and Roth, 1964) suffering from "brain failure" (Isaacs and Caird, 1976). Moreover, an individual of any age might benefit from training and improve his performance even in the absence of any deficit. Are age differences smaller under one condition than under another? is a frequent question in laboratory investigations. In spite of the focus in gerontological research on the nature of the interaction between age and an experimental variable, it is important to realize that an experimental variable does not need to interact with age in order to affect the performance of an older individual (Arenberg and

Robertson, 1974; Schonfield, in press). For example, Monge and Hultsch (1971) found in a paired-associate, rote learning study, that age interacts with the anticipation interval (time-to-respond), but not with the inspection interval (presentation time); however, performance was better at all ages with longer inspection intervals.

Studies of cognitive functioning, as well as intervention strategies, have tended to focus on verbal processes. Future studies, it is hoped, will pay more attention to nonverbal psychomotor skills, since motor activity is frequently an integral part of decreased competence in activities of daily living. One reason that practice has been the major strategy for improving psychomotor decision time and response time may be the nature of skilled behavior. The essence of a skill is that components are integrated into automatic behaviors, and only during acquisition of a new skill is one aware of the various components. Unlike the identification of elements in a verbal learning task, "thinking aloud" is less helpful in isolating the components of a motor task. Possibly a more careful analysis of the qualitative aspects of the initial acquisition of a psychomotor skill would help elucidate the nature of control processes.

It may be useful to distinguish between episodic memory, the memory of a temporally-tagged isolated happening (Tulving, 1972), and generic memory, the memory of general rules or overlearned generalizations which have no special temporal reference (Schonfield and Stones, 1978). Although experimental intervention studies have focused on remediation of the acquisition of new, discrete information (episodic memory), geriatric rehabilitation to increase or restore competence or independence is likely to require modification of generic memories, in addition to learning of new strategies. In this case, the practitioner must confront negative transfer from previously overlearned responses, and surely unlearning is involved. Meichenbaum's (1974) self-instructional strategy training may prove useful as a technique to manage "unlearning."

One final point will be made with respect to age and cognitive skill training. Practitioners or investigators should appreciate and exploit individual differences in teaching new behaviors, or modification of overlearned skills, to elderly individuals. Where preferences for specific control processes are already established, for example, encoding using visual imagery, individuals should be encouraged, if it is appropriate, to apply their preferred strategy. It seems critical for older individuals to use their generic memories in encoding to avoid conditions of information overload (Robertson-Tchabo, Hausman, and Arenberg, 1976). Such overload can result if an individual is required to learn an unfamiliar encoding strategy to learn new information.

SUMMARY AND CONCLUSIONS

Longitudinal data from several experimental laboratory tasks of learning, visual memory, and problem solving, consistently have shown mean declines in performance particularly for persons in their seventies. The evidence for age changes in performance on experimental laboratory tasks does not, in any substantial way, contradict the findings from cross-sectional, experimental studies of age differences in cognitive processing. Nevertheless, even in the 70-year-old group, not all individuals' performances decline. Furthermore, we do not know the practical significance of even substantial decrements in task performance.

Moreover, the view that there are age changes in cognitive processing does not mean that a performance level cannot be modified. Although neuronal loss is currently irreversible, compensation for some cognitive deficits through more effective use of control processes is possible. It would be helpful to clarify, rather than to obscure, the role of organic factors in age-related cognitive deficits.

We certainly agree with Schaie (see Chapter 4) that indexes of the level of cognitive functioning are useful to the extent that they are related to behaviors of social consequence. Assessment and evaluation of an individual's cognitive performance may bear directly on issues such as mandatory retirement, educability and job retraining, and maintenance of independence.

REFERENCES

Anastasi, A. *Psychological Testing,* 4th ed. New York: Macmillan Publishing Co., Inc., 1976.

Arenberg, D. A longitudinal study of problem solving in adults. *J. Gerontol.* **29**:650–658 (1974).

Arenberg, D. Differences and changes with age in the Benton Visual Retention Test. *J. Gerontol.* **33**:534–540 (1978).

Arenberg, D. The Baltimore Longitudinal Study. Paper presented at the 87th Convention of the American Psychological Association, New York, 1979.

Arenberg, D. Memory and learning do decline late in life. In *Proceedings, Aging: A Challenge for Science and Social Policy.* Oxford: Oxford University S. M. Grabowski and W. D. Mason (eds.), *Education for the Aging.* Syracuse: Press, Inc., (in press).

Arenberg, D., and Robertson, E. A. The older individual as a learner. In Eric Clearing House on Adult Education, 1974, pp. 2–39.

Arenberg, D., and Robertson-Tchabo, E. A. Learning and aging. In J. E. Birren and K. W. Schaie (eds.), *Handbook of the Psychology of Aging.* New York: Van Nostrand Reinhold Co., 1977, pp. 421–449.

Atkinson, R. C., and Shiffrin, R. M. Human memory: a proposed system and its control processes. In K. W. Spence and J. T. Spence (eds.), *Advances in the Psychology of Learning and Motivation Research and Theory.* Vol. II. New York: Academic Press, Inc., 1968, pp. 90–197.

Baltes, P. B., and Schaie, K. W. The myth of the twilight years. *Psychol. Today* March:35–40 (1974).

Baltes, P. B., and Schaie, K. W. On the plasticity of intelligence in adulthood and old age: where Horn and Donaldson fail. *Amer. Psychol.* **31**:720–725 (1976).

Benton, A. L. *The Revised Visual Retention Test: Clinical and Experimental Applications,* 3rd ed. New York: Psychological Corporation, 1963.

Botwinick, J. Intellectual abilities. In J. E. Birren and K. W. Schaie (eds.), *Handbook of the Psychology of Aging.* New York: Van Nostrand Reinhold Co., 1977, pp. 580–605.

Cattell, R. B. *Abilities: Their Structure, Growth and Action.* Boston: Houghton Mifflin Co., 1971.

Cyr, J., and Stones, M. J. Performance on cognitive tasks in predicting the behavioral competences in the institutionalized elderly. *Exp. Aging Res.* **3**:253–264 (1977).

Eysenck, M. W. *Human Memory: Theory, Research, and Individual Differences.* Oxford: Pergamon Press, Inc., 1977.

Gilbert, J. G. Thirty-five-year follow-up study of intellectual functioning. *J. Gerontol.* **28**:68–72 (1973).

Hertzog, C., Schaie, K. W., and Gribben, K. Cardiovascular disease and changes in intellectual functioning from middle to old age. *J. Gerontol.* **33**:872–883 (1978).

Horn, J. L., and Donaldson, G. On the myth of intellectual decline in adulthood. *Amer. Psychol.* **31**:701–719 (1976).

Isaacs, B., and Caird, F. I. Brain failure: a contribution to the terminology of mental abnormality in old age. *Age Ageing* **5**:241–244 (1976).

Kahn, R. L., Goldfarb, A. E., Pollack, M., and Peck, A. Brief objective measures for the determination of mental status in the aged. *Amer. J. Psychiat.* **117**:326–328 (1960).

Kahn, R. L., Zarit, S. H., Hilbert, N. M., and Niederhe, M. A. Memory complaint and impairment in the aged: the effect of depression and altered brain function. *Arch. Gen. Psychiat.* **32**:1569–1573 (1975).

Kay, D. W., Beamish, P., and Roth, M. Old age mental disorder in Newcastle upon Tyne. Part I: A study of prevalence. *Br. J. Psychiat.* **110**:146–158 (1964).

Kintsch, W. *Learning, Memory, and Conceptual Processes.* New York: John Wiley & Sons, Inc., 1970.

Lowenthal, M. F., Berkman, P. L., Buehler, J. A., Pierce, R. C., Robinson, B. C., and Trier, M. L. *Aging and Mental Disorder in San Francisco.* San Francisco: Jossey-Bass, Inc., Publishers, 1967.

Mahoney, M. J. *Cognition and Behavior Modification.* Cambridge, Mass.: Ballinger Publishing Company, 1974.

Meichenbaum, D. Self-instructional strategy training: a cognitive prosthesis for the aged. *Human Develop.* **17**:273–280 (1974).

Meichenbaum, D. *Cognitive Behavior Modification.* New York: Plenum Press, 1977.

Melton, A. W., and Martin, E. (eds.) *Coding Processes in Human Memory.* New York: John Wiley & Sons, Inc., 1972.

Monge, R., and Hultsch, D. Paired-associate learning as a function of adult age and the length of the anticipation and inspection intervals. *J. Gerontol.* **26**:157–162 (1971).

Neisser, U. *Cognitive Psychology.* New York: Appleton-Century-Crofts, 1967.

Perlin, S., and Butler, R. N. Psychiatric aspects of adaptation to the aging experience. In J. E. Birren, R. N. Butler, S. W. Greenhouse, L. Sokoloff, and M. R. Yarrow (eds.), *Human Aging: A Biological and Behavioral Study.* USPHS Publ. No. 986. Washington, D.C.: U.S. Government Printing Office, 1963.

Robertson-Tchabo, E. A., Arenberg, D., and Costa, P. T., Jr. Temperamental predictors of longitudinal change in performance on the Benton Revised Visual Retention Test among seventy year old men: an exploratory study. In F. Hoffmeister and C. Müller (eds.), *Brain Function in Old Age.* Proceedings, Bayer Symposium, 7th. Berlin: Springer-Verlag, New York, Inc., 1979, pp. 151–159.

Robertson-Tchabo, E. A., Hausman, C., and Arenberg, D. A classical mnemonic for older learners. *Educ. Gerontol.* **1**:215–226 (1976).

Schaie, K. W., and Baltes, P. B. Some faith helps to see the forest: a final comment on the Horn and Donaldson myth on the Baltes-Schaie position on adult intelligence. *Amer. Psychol.* **32**:1118–1120 (1977).

Schaie, K. W., Labouvie, G. V., and Buech, B. U. Generational and cohort-specific differences in adult cognitive functioning: a fourteen-year study of independent samples. *Develop. Psychol.* **9**:151–166 (1973).

Schaie, K. W., and Labouvie-Vief, G. V. Generational versus ontogenetic

components of change in adult cognitive behavior: a fourteen-year cross-sequential study. *Develop. Psychol.* **10**:305–320 (1974).
Schaie, K. W., and Strother, C. R. A cross-sequential study of age changes in cognitive behavior. *Psychol. Bull.* **70**:671–680 (1968a).
Schaie, K. W., and Strother, C. R. The effect of time and cohort differences upon age changes in cognitive behavior. *Multivar. Behav. Res.* **3**:259–294 (1968b).
Schonfield, D. Learning and memory. In J. E. Birren and K. W. Schaie (eds.), *Handbook on Mental Health and Aging*. New York: Van Nostrand Reinhold Co. (in press).
Schonfield, D., and Stones, M. J. Remembering and aging. In J. F. Kihlstrom and F. J. Evans (eds.), *Functional Disorders of Memory*. New York: Halsted Press, 1978.
Tulving, E. Episodic and semantic memory. In E. Tulving and W. Donaldson (eds.), *Organization of Memory*. New York: Academic Press, Inc., 1972.

8
Summary

Richard L. Sprott

*The Jackson Laboratory
Bar Harbor, Maine*

There are large gaps in our knowledge of the normal course of development of learning abilities, cognition, and intelligence. The frustrations of each of the contributors to this volume are obvious to, and perhaps shared by, the reader. This is a positive state of affairs, however, and is certainly an improvement over the almost total ignorance and complacency which existed in many quarters only a decade or two ago. If you, the reader, share some of our frustration over contradictory results, lack of agreement on basic issues, and uninspired research, then we have accomplished a portion of our goals. Behavioral gerontology is an infant science, facing a challenge to contribute meaningfully to human understanding. We will be able to meet this challenge only by devoting research talent, money, and space to the effort. The infusion of new young talent into the field in the last decade has already had a noticeable effect. It is hoped that the next decade will see a comparable growth not only in research quantity, but in research quality as well.

While all of the contributors emphasized the controversial aspects of their research and the questions which remain to be answered, there are many areas of agreement as well. In a broad sense there is agreement that the terms learning, cognition, and intelligence each encompass a spectrum of abilities. The increasing attention gerontologists are giving to separate consideration of individual abilities within each spectrum is one of the promising signs of maturation of the field. Increased specification of the particular behavior or ability under investigation should reduce the number of fruitless arguments which arise when investigators argue points from different sets of limited data. Such arguments have been particularly common in the area of human intelligence where the interest of the public, Congress, and the press is high and pressure for global assessments is intense.

There are also areas of considerable agreement for some specific behaviors and abilities. The overwhelming weight of data on voluntary activity shows that mice, rats, and men become less active as they age. The rate of decline can be modified by experience or environmental manipulation, but the fact that decline occurs is clear. The universality of this observation makes it clear that declining activity is a direct consequence of biological changes in aging organisms. We may be able to affect the rate somewhat by manipulating environmental and motivational factors, but declining activity levels will remain a fact of life until we find and are able to modify the rate-limiting physiological factors.

The ability of mice and rats to perform difficult motor tasks as well as the response speed and motor skill of aging human subjects show the same type of decline from maturity onward. Here the physiological changes are more obvious and are related to changes in muscle tissue and muscle-to-lipid ratios (Shephard, 1978). Changes in the peripheral and central nervous systems may also be involved, particularly in response-speed decrements, but these changes are not yet as well understood.

Since virtually all investigators agree that activity levels and motor skills decline, why does research on these factors continue? There are two primary reasons. Both factors are important components of performance in most test situations for other abilities. While we all agree on the necessity to account for activity, response-speed, and motor-skill variables, there is no generally agreed-upon solution to the problem. In addition, there is some disagreement as to whether these factors are really just performance variables or are in fact a part of the ability we seek to measure. As Dr. Schaie points out in his chapter, one's conviction on this point depends on the definition of ability or intelligence one assumes. If "latent" ability is the criterion, then these variables are confounding elements and they should be eliminated or minimized. On the other hand, if competence is the criterion, then these variables may be important to assessment. Even in the latter situation, however, it is still important to delineate the degree to which competence rests upon such variables.

There is also quite general agreement that some types of learning abilities in mice, rats and human beings remain intact throughout normal life spans in healthy individuals. Mice and rats retain the ability to learn simple mazes and operant tasks until shortly before they die. Decrements in performance in these situations, when observed, are important signals of impending morbidity, the rodent equivalent of "terminal drop." Similarly, most investigators agree that some types of human learning abilities are preserved until terminal pathologies progress to the point of interference with homeostatic function. These abilities include simple learning tasks comparable to those used in rodent tests and the class of abilities which underlie what Schaie and others call "crystallized intelligence." That these abilities tend to be heavily culture-laden, that is dependent upon range of vocabulary, number facility, or stores of general information, has complicated discussion of their relevance to the physiological changes which are presumed to underlie decline with aging. While the research questions posed by this debate are important, they should not be permitted to obscure the fact that, for these types of abilities, little or no decrement is observed throughout the life spans of healthy individuals.

The primary area of continuing controversy is that of complex learning. The arguments are the same in the animal literature as in the human intelligence literature because the problems are similar, and the data show the same inconsistencies. At the same time, the opinions of most investigators are not as different as they appear at first glance. Most of us agree that performance in many complex learning situations declines with advancing age. Our arguments are over the causes of declining performance and their relevance to "latent" abilities. The question of whether it is possible to measure complex abilities in the absence of the confounding influences of impaired health, changing motivations, and cultural effects upon successive cohorts has not yet been settled. Until there is at least some general agreement upon acceptable approaches to these problems, the debates will continue.

Finally, there appears to be fairly general acceptance of the fact that some abilities change as a result of entrance into a developmental stage characteristic of older individuals. The questions of behavioral rigidity and caution depend upon assumptions of developmental changes which affect personality and ability. Many investigators assume that characteristic senile changes occur in the brain or some of its parts, which impair functioning in ways which produce rigidity and caution by interfering with the individual's ability to process information. So far, research with animal models has produced little, if any, reliable evidence of similar changes in rats and mice. The relevance of the lack of such changes in rodents to human problems is still an open question. It is certainly true that rodents have simpler nervous systems which are not as influenced by cortical factors as those of human beings. It may also be true that we have not yet found ways to measure "personality" changes in mice, if they in fact exist. What we can conclude with some confidence is that there does not appear to be a developmental program, inherent in genes and common to mammals, which makes changes like rigidity a property of advanced age. Whether such a genetic program exists for all, or most, human individuals is a question which probably cannot be answered by research on lower organisms.

Among the major questions which are likely to be the focus of research in the immediate future, a few stand out. The question of the importance of health status is the most obvious of these, since it is central to many other research questions and is at the same time a matter of considerable public concern. Health status could affect measured abilities in at least two ways. First, debilitating disease states reduce performance levels in many situations as is clearly shown in the preceding chapters. Second, and perhaps more important, some disease states have effects which reduce latent abilities by interfering with the functions of the central nervous system. It is important to differentiate "normal" changes, that is changes in the absence of disease processes, from those which result from health impairment. Most investigators are aware of the possible confounding effects of poor health in one direction only. That is, they are aware that poor health may reduce performance levels and thereby lead to erroneous conclusions of ability decrements. It is equally important, as Elias points out, to realize that impaired health may be a non-causal correlate of performance decline. Thus, the presence of debilitating disease may be one of several indicators of a more general loss of homeostatic function. As our society considers approaches and commitments to national health programs, it is important that we not fail to take steps which will be of genuine benefit to our population, including the elderly. At the same time, it is also important that we not promise benefits which cannot be delivered.

The origins and extent of motivational changes will continue to be a major concern of behavioral gerontologists. Some changes seem normal, such as declining interest in social status, and are assumed to result from cultural expectations. Others, like declining interest in exercise, also seem normal, but are assumed to reflect physiological changes. Neither of these examples is simple, as it is possible to construct a logical physiological or cultural explanation for each of them. The discovery of hypothalamic control centers for many behaviors has shown that functional disturbances to relatively small, discrete regions of the brain can have profound effects upon motivation. It is also obvious that cultural expectations may have equally profound effects. Whether the cultural expectations are conditioned by social, economic, and political considerations or by cultural exposure to physiological imperatives is often difficult to determine. In fact, the two types of influence are probably intertwined in most cases.

As behavioral gerontologists become more confident of a continuing place in the spectrum of scientific disciplines which receives support and recognition from the federal government, the public, and their colleagues, increasing numbers of bright young scientists should enter the field. This infusion of competition and new ideas should in turn lead to more discriminating research approaches, a sharpening of the questions posed and the projects undertaken. We are probably reaching the end of a period of concentration upon methodological issues. The concern was a natural and proper response to a history of research which lacked rigor and which therefore contributed more confusion than enlightenment. Students in the area are now far better trained and investigators are more aware of the influences of confounding variables than they were a decade ago. It is important now that we use our increasing resources wisely to address significant research questions. Research on aging, whether it is conducted with animal models or human populations, is enormously expensive in terms of time and money, but interest in this research is currently high and rapidly rising. We should not waste our opportunity while we have it.

In simple terms, the task before us is to determine which human and animal abilities remain intact as aging progresses and which do not. In those cases where abilities usually are preserved, this information needs to be made generally available so that policy decisions and cultural expectations can match reality and are not used to impose artificial restrictions upon competent individuals, and so that appropriate treatment strategies can be devised for the "exceptional" individuals who suffer decrements. In cases where ability decrements are normal concomitants of aging, this information is also important to policymakers and to individuals trying to make rational decisions about their futures.

As some of the contributors have pointed out, the separation of abilities from other performance variables is not a simple matter. The answers to some of our questions are not likely to be found in behavior laboratories. One of the noticeable differences between behavioral gerontology and many other areas of scientific inquiry is the lack of interdisciplinary research. In order to address the health issue, motivation issues, and the role of genetic programs of development, we will have to foster interdisciplinary research. The input of pathologists, physiologists, geneticists, and biochemists into the design, conduct, and analysis of behavioral research should be encouraged. Interdisciplinary research will have the added benefit of freeing behavioral gerontology from the traditional narrow focus of American psychology, which tends to treat behavior as a set of processes separate from the biological organisms which emit the behaviors.

While the debate among biological gerontologists about the existence and nature of inborn "clocks" which determine the life spans of organisms has effects upon research assumptions made by investigators of learning abilities and intelligence, it is not one of our major concerns. Our concern is more with the quality of life than with its length. To be sure, we would all like to live as long as possible, but none of us wish to become a burden to ourselves, our families or our society. The major benefit to be derived from an understanding of the developmental courses of abilities and intelligence should be the development of rational expectations and therapies for aging individuals, which permit as many of us as possible to live useful lives and age gracefully.

REFERENCES

Shephard, R. J. Exercise and aging. In J. A. Behnke, C. E. Finch, and G. B. Moment (eds.), *The Biology of Aging*. New York: Plenum Press, 1978, pp. 131–149.

Index

Index

Index

Abrahams study (1976), 106
Active-avoidance conditioning, 11–12
Aging
    and age differences and changes as predictors of cognitive competence, 149–150
    and arguments over normalcy, 1, 2
    and decline in sensory and motor skills, 2
    and difficulty in measuring ability and intelligence, 3–4
    and effects of health status on intelligence, 68–69
    and learning behavior in mice, 25–38
    and learning in rodent research, 5–25
    and Primary Mental Abilities Test, 56–68
    and psychometric vs. information-processing approaches to cognition, 150–152
    and vascular diseases and cognitive performance, 107–110
    and WAIS data on intelligence, 54–56
Alcohol studies in mice, 124
Animal model systems, 27
    advantage of, 34
    in hypertension research, 115–117
Army Alpha Test, 43
Avoidance learning, 6, 10–12, 21, 35

Baltimore Longitudinal Study, 143, 149
Baltimore Longitudinal Study of Aging (BLSA), 143, 144, 145, 147
Behavioral gerontology
    history of empirical work in, 42–45
    and hypertension research, 86–88, 93–98, 107–110
    and issues in behavioral research, 45–52
    and major issues of rat gerontology, 26–29
    problem of methodology in, 2, 4, 162
    state of the art, 158–163
Behavioral research. *See* Studies, behavioral.
Behavioral studies. *See* Studies, behavioral.
Benton Visual Retention Test, 143, 144
Binet and Simon study (1908), 44
Binet Intelligence Test, 43
Birkhill and Schaie study (1975), 72
Blum, Fossnage and Jarvik study (1972), 56
Botwinick and Storandt study (1974), 80
Botwinick, Brinley, and Robbin studies, 9
Botwinick studies, 6

Cardiovascular disease 82, 89–93, 105–106, 114
Carr maze, 6
Category Test, 99, 102
Cattell, J. Mck. study (1890), 44
Cattell study (1971), 152
Cerebral blood flow and cognitive performance, 106–107
Cerebrovascular disorders, 89–93
Cognition, 140, 150–152
Cognitive functioning
    See also Intelligence.

165

166 Index

Cognitive functioning (*cont.*)
  age differences and changes as predictors of, 149–150
  information processing models of, 150–152
  longitudinal studies on, 142–148
  modifiability of, 152–154
  psychometric approach to, 150–152
  self-report studies in, 141–142
  as a term, 140
Cognitive performance. *See* Cognitive functioning.
Cognitive skill training, 150, 153
Connolly and Bruner study (1974), 44
Cornell Medical Index, 80
Cross-sectional research design, 142
Cultural expectations. *See* Societal expectations.

Data bases for studying intelligence, 48–50
Demographic factors influencing intelligence, 68
Doppelt and Wallace study (1955), 54
Doty and O'Hare study, 12
Doty et al. studies, 11–12

Eisdorfer and Wilkie study (1973), 56
Eisdorfer, Busse, and Cohen study (1959), 55
Environmental factors influencing intelligence, 3, 4, 69–70
Enzer, Simonson, and Blankstein study (1942), 101
Essential hypertension. *See* Hypertension, essential.
Eysenck study (1977), 151

Face-Hand Test, 141
Field studies, 6–7
Figural relations, 47
Finger Oscillation Test, 99, 100
Fluid and crystallized intelligence, 47
Freund and Walker study, 34

Galton study (1883), 44
Genetic definition in mouse models, 27, 29, 37
Geneva model of intelligence, 47

Gerontology. *See* Behavioral gerontology.
Goldman and co-workers study (1974), 101
Goodrick studies
  (1967), 35
  (1968), 12
  (1972), 16, 17
  (1973), 18
Guilford study (1967), 44

Hall et al. study (1972), 55
Hall, G. Stanley, 42
Halstead Impairment Index, 101
Halstead-Reitan Neuropsychological Test Battery, 82, 93
  description of various tests in, 98–104
Harwood and Naylor study (1971), 55
Health status (as an influence on behavior), 2
  and intelligence, 68–69
  in behavioral studies, 78–82
  future of in research, 161
Hertzog, Gribbin, and Schaie study (1975), 105
Hertzog, Gribbin, and Schaie study (1978), 103
Hollingsworth, H.L., 42
Horn and Donaldson study (1976), 62
Hypertension
  and biased performance in research, 98
  definition of, 90
  direction for future studies in, 107–110
  research in using animal models, 114–117
  and WAIS data, 96
Hypertension, essential
  and control of nonphysiological variables in study of, 107
  definition of, 83
  and distinction between secondary hypertension, 81
  as a model for insidious disease, 81
  and plasma renin activity, 86
  and WAIS data, 95

Impairment Index, 100, 102

Index of Educational Aptitude, 68
Inductive reasoning, 47
Information-processing view of cognitive function, 150, 151
Intelligence
  See also Cognitive functioning
  and competence, 44–45
  "crystallized," 47, 160
  and current status of question of intellectual decline with age, 70–71
  data bases for study of: age differences vs. age changes, 48–49; experimental mortality, 49; pathological vs. normal aging, 50
  and decline in physical vigor, 41–42
  difficulty in measuring, 3–4, 71–72
  and directions for future studies in hypertension, 107–110
  effect of demographic factors on, 68
  effect of environmental factors on, 69–70
  effect of health history factors on, 68–69
  and health status in behavioral studies, 78–82
  history of empirical work on, 42–45
  and the issue of age decrement among gerontologists, 53–54
  measurement of: age corrected vs. absolute level norms, 50–51; performance vs. potential, 52; speeded vs. power tests, 51–52
  models of: fluid and crystallized, 47; general construct, 46; multi-factor theories, 46–47; stage theories, 47–48
  and Primary Mental Abilities Test data on age changes, 56–68
  and studies of hypertension, 93–98
  and WAIS data on intellectual changes with age, 54–56
International Classification of Diseases (ICDA), 68
Ischemic stroke, 89
Isomorphism between physical vigor and intellectual abilities, 41

Jones and Conrad study (1933), 43
Journal of Gerontology, 78, 79

Kahn and co-workers study (1975), 141
Kay and Sime studies, 8–9

Learning ability
  and avoidance learning, 10–11
  difficulty in measuring, 3–4
  improvement of in rats using massed practice, 21
  land maze learning in rats, 5–7
  in mice, 37–38, 160
  and motor skills in mice, 30–33
  multiple discrimination learning in rats, 7–8
  primary concern of studies in, 1, 2
  and state of the art of behavioral gerontology, 160, 161
Learning behavior in aging mice, 29–38
Lever-escape tests, 6
Life-Complexity Inventory (LCI), 69, 70
Light study (1975), 84, 106
Light study (1978), 89, 106
Logical Memory Test, 103
Longitudinal studies on cognitive functioning, 142–148
Lowenthal, Berkman, and associates study (1967), 141

Maze learning, 6–7, 16, 22, 35
Maze studies, 12–22
Measuring intelligence in adults, 50–52
Meichenbaum study (1974), 153
Memory span, 47
Mental Status Questionnaire, 141
Methodology
  and active-avoidance conditioning, 11
  concern with in behavioral gerontology, 2, 162
  issues in behavioral research, 45–52
  and passive-avoidance conditioning, 11
  problems of in research on aging, 4
  in rat research by Fields, 7
  in rat research by Goodrick, 12–14, 16–20, 22
  in rat research by Kay and Simes, 8–9
  in rat research by Stone, 6–7
  in rat research by Verzar-McDougall, 8
  in speed response studies, 82–93
  in studies of hypertension using mice, 119–133

Index

Mice
  and advantages of genetic definition, 27, 29, 37
  determining behavioral maturity in, 30
  learning ability in, 30–33, 37–38, 159–160
  longevity in, 35
  and maturation effects in learning, 35
  as a model system in research, 27, 29
  motor skills and learning ability in, 30–33, 137–138, 159–160
  selection process of in Schlager's experiments, 117–119
  in studies of hypertension, 115–137
  studies on by Sprott, 11
  studies on by Yerkes and Dodson, 10–11
Miquel and Blasco study, 30–31
Models of intelligence, 46–48
Monge and Hultsch study (1971), 153
Motivation, 2
  in avoidance learning, 10
  future of in behavioral gerontology, 162
  in mice research, 33
  in rat research, 7, 8, 9
Motor skills
  decline in and aging, 2, 159
  in mice research, 30, 31
  and passive-avoidance learning, 35
Multifactor theories of intelligence, 46–47
Multiple-discrimination learning, 7–8
Munn studies, 6

National Institute on Aging, 143

Obrist, Busse, and Henry study, 106
Obrist study (1964), 95
Oliverio and Bovet study (1966), 35
Omnibus tests of intelligence, 46

Passive-avoidance conditioning, 11
Passive-avoidance learning, 35
Perseverative errors, 14, 17, 19
Piaget study (1972), 47
Plasma renin activity (PRA), 86, 87
Pressey, Sydney, 42

Primary Mental Abilities Test, 53, 56, 103, 105
  basic flaw of cross-sectional studies, 57
  data from follow-up studies, 58–63
  effect of attrition on findings in, 63–66
  magnitude of age changes in, 66–68
  results of the first parametric study, 57
Psychological tests, 150
Psychometric tests, 150
Psychometric view of cognitive function, 150–152
Psychomotor activities
  improvement of, 153
  studies of in healthy subjects, 104–105

Rats
  and active-avoidance conditioning task, 11–12
  adequacy of as a model for human learning, 26–27
  analysis of learning process in, 5
  and avoidance learning by age, 10–11
  and behavioral rigidity by age, 9
  and food deprivation and learning by age, 8–9
  learning ability in, 159–160
  learning rate in first 2 years of life, 6
  maze study with, 12–22
  and multiple discrimination learning ability by age, 8
Rehabilitation, 150
Renin, 86
Roderick, Wimer, and Wimer study (1976), 127

Savage, Britton, Bolton, and Hall study (1973), 56
Schaie and Labouvie-Vief study (1974), 143
Schaie and Strother study (1968), 63
Schaie, Labouvie, and Buech study (1973), 63, 143
Scheidt and Schaie study (1978), 72
Schlager, Gunther, 115
Self-report studies on cognitive functioning, 141–142
Senescense, 2
  and learning ability in mice, 37–38

measuring, 4
in mouse research, 30, 35
in rat research, 11, 12
Sensory ability
decline in and aging, 2
and genetic variables in mice, 37
Shepard, 33
Shock-avoidance tests, 21
Shock, electrical, 10
Shuttle box learning, 35
Sime and Kay study (1962), 9
Social aggression study in mice, 124
Societal expectations (as an influence on behavior), 2, 70
Spearman study (1927), 46
Spieth study (1964, 1965), 82, 106
Sprague-Dawley rats, 7
Sprott and Eleftheriou study, 34
Sprott and Stavnes study (1975), 11
Sprott study, 11
Stage theories of adult development, 47–48
Stone, Calvin, 5, 6, 7
Stone monographs, 5–7
Stone 14-unit T-maze
in works of Stone, 6
in Verzar-McDougall study, 8
in Goodrick study, 12, 16
Studies, behavioral
and adequacy of the rat as a model for human learning, 26–27
and cerebral blood flow, 106–107
comparing hypertension patients with cerebrovascular and heart disease patients, 89–93
on cognitive functioning, 141, 148
and data bases for studying intelligence, 48–50
and difficulty in interpreting hypertension research, 88–89
and difficulty in measuring ability and intelligence, 3–4
and elimination of extraneous variables, 30
future of with mice, 134–135
and the Halstead-Reitan test battery, 98–104
and history of empirical work on intelligence, 42–45

in hypertension research, 86–88, 93–98, 107–110
of hypertension in mice, 115–137
and learning ability, 2
of learning behavior in aging mice, 27–29, 35–38
on lower animals, 3
and maturation effects, 35
in mice physiology, 133
in mice by Sprott, 11
in mice by Yerkes and Dodson, 10–11
and models of intelligence, 46–47
of psychomotor performance in healthy subjects, 104–105
in rats by Botwinick, Brinley, and Robbin, 9
in rats by Fields, 7–8
in rats by Kay and Simes, 8–9
in rats by Stone, 5–7
in rats by Verzar-McDougall, 8
of relationship of cardiovascular disease and speed response, 82–86
of social agression in mice, 124
and state of the art of behavioral gerontology, 158–163
using alcohol in mice, 124
using corticosterone in mice, 125
Szafran studies, 104

Tactual Performance Test, 99, 100, 101, 102
Terman study (1916), 43
Thompson, Eisdorfer, and Estes study (1970), 105
Three plate-escape problem, 6
Thurstone study (1938), 46
TPT-memory test, 99, 103
Trail-Making Test, 99, 102
Transient ischemic attack (TIA), 89

Vascular diseases and cognitive performance, 107–110
Verzar-McDougall study, 8
Visual Reproduction Test, 103

Water maze learning, 35, 121
WAIS Symbol-Substitution Task, 82
Wechsler Adult Intelligence Test (WAIS), 52

170 Index

Wechsler Adult Intelligence Test (*cont.*)
   data on intellectual changes with age, 54–56
   in studies of hypertension, 94–98
Wechsler-Bellevue Intelligence Test, 43
Wilkie and co-workers (1976), 103
Wilkie and Eisdorfer study (1971), 93, 97, 106
Wilkie, Eisdorfer, and Nowlin study (1976), 103
Wissler study (1901), 44

Wood, Elias, Schultz, and Pentz study (1978), 80
Wood, Elias, Schultz, and Pentz study (1979), 98
Wood, Gibson W., 122

Yerkes and Dodson study, 10
Yerkes study (1921), 43
Y-maze
   and learning differences by age, 9